Heart Expressions from the Throne Room

Heart Expressions from the Throne Room

Awakening God's Beloved on the College Campus

Sjhira Ellzey

Heart Expressions from the Throne Room

Jenson Stanley Publishing

Copyright © 2020 Sjhira Ellzey

All rights reserved. No part of this book may be used or reproduced by any means, graphic, electronic, or mechanical, including photocopying, recording, taping or by any information storage retrieval system without the written permission of the publisher except in the case of brief quotations embodied in critical articles and reviews.

Unless otherwise noted, Scripture are taken from THE HOLY BIBLE, ENGLISH STANDARD VERSION (ESV): Scriptures taken from THE HOLY BIBLE, ENGLISH STANDARD VERSION ® Copyright© 2001 by Crossway, a publishing ministry of Good News Publishers. Used by permission.

Scriptures marked NIV are taken from the NEW INTERNATIONAL VERSION (NIV): Scripture taken from THE HOLY BIBLE, NEW INTERNATIONAL VERSION ®. Copyright© 1973, 1978, 1984, 2011 by Biblica, Inc.TM. Used by permission of Zondervan

Scriptures marked NKJV are taken from the NEW KING JAMES VERSION (NKJV): Scripture taken from the NEW KING JAMES VERSION®. Copyright© 1982 by Thomas Nelson, Inc. Used by permission. All rights reserved.

Scriptures marked NLT are taken from the HOLY BIBLE, NEW LIVING TRANSLATION (NLT): Scriptures taken from the HOLY BIBLE, NEW LIVING TRANSLATION, Copyright© 1996, 2004, 2007 by Tyndale House Foundation. Used by permission of Tyndale House Publishers, Inc., Carol Stream, Illinois 60188. All rights reserved. Used by permission.

Scriptures marked AMPC are taken from the AMPLIFIED BIBLE Classic Edition (AMPC): Scripture taken from the AMPLIFIED® BIBLE, Copyright © 1954, 1958, 1962, 1964, 1965, 1987 by the Lockman Foundation Used by Permission. (www.Lockman.org)

Scripture quotations marked TPT are from The Passion Translation®. Copyright © 2017, 2018 by Passion & Fire Ministries, Inc. Used by permission. All rights reserved. ThePassionTranslation.com.

Book Cover Design was done by Rick Schroeppel
www.2020bookcoverdesign.com

DEDICATION

This book was inspired by the Holy Spirit. When I thought its purpose was lost and dead He breathed and I was reminded of the power of purpose being fulfilled. Therefore, I wholeheartedly dedicate this book to the Lord, God Almighty.

ACKNOWLEDGMENTS

When you decide to take on a new venture, such as writing a book, it can be very intimidating and overwhelming. Before I proceed, I have to acknowledge certain people God has placed in my life that helped cheer me on as this dream turned into reality. Kyndl, you are the cheerleading captain. The kind of support you give is what causes eagles to not only fly, but soar. You, my love, ignite me to new heights.

My precious little Jenson, when I look into your eyes I see my Jesus, and when you place your hand on my cheek I feel His touch.

Mom, you've been there for me since day 1, literally, and believed in the importance of my little life before taking one look at my face. Thank you for being my first introduction to The Way.

Daddy, your words in those final hours, "Keep talking, I'm listening," unlocked something in me. Thank you for affirming that I have a voice worthy of being heard.

Nina Donnell, I'm wondering when your picture will be placed next to the definition of "God-mother." You love and support with such purity and selflessness. I can only imagine what your reward in Glory will be like.

Eleanor Graves, from the moment I met you; your beautiful smile, arms stretched out and your warm embrace, I knew you were being placed as a foundational stepping stone into my destiny.

To the following women: Ashley Mills, Erica Nork, Ladonna Parham, Megan Van Zyl, Michelle Meskel, and Novella Dean, your prayers were wind behind my back as I crossed the finish line of this book writing/publishing marathon.

Donna Christopher, I thank you for taking on this project; editing, formatting and helping me navigate through all the details of self-publishing. Your guidance has truly been a breath of fresh air.

Rick Schroeppel, working with you on the cover design was a delight. Your expertise mixed with a God-given gift shines through and I couldn't be more pleased.

Carolyn Oliver, McKenna Morgan and the ladies at Oral Roberts University and the Kings College, thank you for taking time to give your helpful feedback.

Jerry and Charlene, "Team Turney," a cheering section is incomplete without your voices. Thank you for wanting to spread the word about this book before I was even ready and Charlene for taking my first author's bio photo.

A very special thank you to all the women who opened up your hearts to me; whose stories are shared in this book. Your honest reflections and thoughts add depth by revealing the personal and intimate heart of God.

Last but not least, thank you to everyone who has ever believed in me and encouraged me in my relationship with Jesus. There are so many and I appreciate each and every one of you.

CONTENTS

Introduction   i

PART I
The Appetizer
Preparing the Heart to Receive

Inspiration, Despair & Renewal	3
A Divine Valentine	11
Perspective Shift	17
Hearing by Faith & Drenched by Love	28

PART II
The Main Course
Heart Expressions from the Throne Room

1.	I Will Wait for You	42
2.	Hours, Minutes, and Seconds	46
3.	Precious Thoughts	49
4.	Magnificent Beauty	52
5.	My Heart at Rest	56
6.	When You Said, "Yes"	60
7.	Lovesick	64
8.	Rose Petals	68
9.	Joy	72
10.	Close to You	76
11.	One True Love	80
12.	Form and Feature	84
13.	I am Near	88
14.	Lift Your Eyes	92
15.	Hidden Treasure	95
16.	Sweetness	99

17. The Perfect Sunset	103
18. Speechless…Breathless	107
19. Knight in Shining Armor	111
20. Awakened by Beauty	115
21. Just Me and You	118
22. I Danced	121
23. Softly Kiss You	125
24. Lovely	128
25. Your Tears	132
26. For an Eternity	136
27. Beautiful Bride	140
28. Love Language	144
29. Elegance	148
30. Gaze in Wonder	152
31. Romanced	155
32. Together as One	159
33. I Will Carry You	163
34. Hold My Hand	167
35. Radiant	171
36. Mystery to Behold	175

PART III
The Dessert
Personal Stories from College Women

Lauryn	182
Tiffany	185
Melissa	189
Mia	191
Sonya	194
Renee	198
Nicole	201
Felicia	203

Courtney	205
Willow	208
Norah	211
Elise	214
Victoria	217
Cynthia	222
Yolanda	226
Hailee	228
Morgan	231
Amanda	237
Karyn	241
Mikaela	245
Charlotte	250
Crystal	255
Brianna	259
Ellen	262
Tasha	264
Angelique	267
Dee Dee	273
Tori	277
Parting Words	281
About the Author	284

~ INTRODUCTION ~

You're in college, congratulations! Your parents/guardians have taken a backseat to much of your decision making and you are "on your own." The culture you are surrounded by is different than home life: no parents, community bathrooms, sharing a room with a complete stranger, pulling an all-nighter in the dorm lobby, bar crawls, fraternity/sorority parties, 2am food binges, sex across the hall, skipping class without a doctor's note, and huge lecture halls designed to "weed out" the unworthy. It is apparent that many, if not most of your peers have no desire to pursue a relationship with God, and now that you have the choice, sleeping in Sunday morning sounds way more appealing than nodding off in a boring church service. And for those of you attending college in a new and unfamiliar town, the thought of going on a church hunt may be exhausting.

I get it. I've been there. As a Christian woman on a college campus you feel a tug to live for Jesus but may question what that looks like given your surroundings. Going through the motions of weekly church or Bible study attendance is not quenching the thirst. There has to be more! The Lord knows. He cares deeply about this specific time in your life. He cares deeply about you. Thoughts of you consume His heart and He wants to reveal himself to you.

While reading this book you will hear the heart of God in the form of love notes; in ways you may have never heard or imagined. The book is divided into three sections: the appetizer, the main course, and the dessert.

The appetizer sets the tone for the entire meal. You will hear some of my personal stories, including how this book came to be. This section will leave you hungry and wanting more; preparing your appetite (your heart) for the main course.

The main course is the meat and potatoes (or tofu for the vegetarians). This is where you will hear the beautiful Heart Expressions from the Throne

Room. Take time to chew on the content. Savor the different flavors before swallowing and digesting. A personal reflection space is included for you to interact with the Lord and write down what He is speaking to you. What additional scriptures come to mind? Maybe He will speak in the form of pictures or a song. Whatever it is, record it in the blank space provided.

Once your love tank is filled up it will be time for dessert and, trust me, there is always room for dessert! In this section you will enjoy sweet stories of how the very heart expressions from the main course impacted a group of young ladies on the college campus. Indulge in the gooey love of Jesus as His Spirit overflows into your pores.

This book is NOT to replace the Bible. Instead, I hope for it to awaken and stir up your desire for love; prompting you to read the Word of God with a fresh sense of wonder and awe. This is about your heart being ravished beyond normal comprehension. This is about allowing a mysterious fascination to consume your inner most being. This is not about going to church. This is about being the Church; a unique portion of the intricate body of Christ. This is not about attending a weekly Bible study. This is about being famished for the Word of God and the incredible satisfaction it brings when you partake of it. This is not about feeling comfortable, or safe, or important within a Christian clique. This is about laying your life down at the feet of Jesus in total surrender and not caring if you look foolish. This is about a lost and dying world that is looking for a savior. This is about the heart. He wants you to know His heart and how it beats for you. It has always been and will forever be about the heart. The perfect and most beautiful heart of God!

> *As they were eating, Jesus took some bread and blessed it. Then he broke it in pieces and gave it to the disciples, saying, "Take this and eat it, for this is my body." And he took a cup of wine and gave thanks to God for it. He gave it to them and said, "Each of you drink from it, for this is my blood, which confirms the covenant between God and his people. It is poured out as a sacrifice to forgive the sins of many (Matthew 26:26-28 NLT).*

Part I
The Appetizer

Preparing the Heart to Receive

*Oh, taste and see that the Lord is good!
(Psalm 34:8).*

Heart Expressions from the Throne Room

In a moment you are about to enjoy some tasty hors d'oeuvres. I am first going to share a snapshot of my story and how this book came to be. Then, your appetite will be stimulated as I offer some practical ways to prepare for the main course. This portion sets the tone for the entire feast, so relax and take your time. Bon Appetit!

Sjhira Ellzey

INSPIRATION, DESPAIR, AND RENEWAL

As a college student pursuing a career in medicine, my heart felt a strong tug in another direction; vocational ministry – college campus ministry to be exact. One month after graduation I moved to California to complete seminary coursework through Fuller Theological Seminary and "on-the-job" training at the University of Southern California. Once the coursework was completed, I went back to my hometown in Chicago where I raised a full support team. This team consisted of men, women, and churches who invested in me financially and prayerfully so I could focus on the work God called me to do. These people were a constant source of encouragement and I am eternally grateful for their vital role in my journey.

For three and a half years I worked as a vocational campus missionary sharing the gospel and ministering to college students. Several of my ministry opportunities took place on campuses around the world, however, my home base was Nashville, TN. It was there I spent most of my time, and the two campuses that received a constant outpouring of my heart and soul were Fisk University and Tennessee State University (TSU). The inspiration to write this book was birthed while serving the students on these two campuses.

In February 2007 the Lord gave me an idea; a way to bless the young women who attended our weekly campus Bible studies. This idea resulted in a powerful move of the Holy Spirit. The Lord then told me to collect stories from the students involved and put everything in book form. I was extremely zealous about writing a book and immediately began the interviews. Then the inevitable happened; life got busy, I got distracted, and the writing slowed down until it came to a complete stop. My zealous sentiments had become overwhelmed. The longer it took for me to resume writing, the harder it was. And so, my binder filled with inspiring stories, notes, and awesome proof of a passionate God ended up in a wicker basket at the foot of my bed.

Two years later, my call to vocational campus ministry came to an end and I moved across town. The move was a disaster and entirely my fault. My old lease ended in May and my new one began in August. During the 2 months of June and July I was traveling and failed to secure proper storage space. To make a long story short, a lot of my stuff was either thrown out or given away.

Upon returning to Nashville to move into my new home I had to face the consequences of my poor decision. The bags of clothes and the cool tiered shelf from Pier 1 were missed, but I got over them pretty quickly. What caused my heart to sink and the blood to rush out of my face was discovering that the wicker basket was gone. I desperately searched my remaining items for the notebook to no avail. I even prayed that God would miraculously transport it out of a garbage dump and back into my hands.

When nothing happened I felt lower than low, defeated, and extremely irresponsible. All I could think was God told me to write a book and I couldn't write it without my notes, therefore, I had completely failed Him. I wondered why He asked me to do this in the first place if He knew I wouldn't follow through. Eventually I came to terms with reality and stopped beating myself up. Knowing that God had moved mightily on the campuses of Fisk and TSU, impacting many students' lives for His glory, was good enough. Besides, I would still be able to share the story in general terms. And so, I moved forward in the confidence of God's mercy.

As I have planned, so shall it be, and as I have purposed, so shall it stand (Isaiah 14:24).

In April 2017 my husband, Kyndl, and I had just closed on our first home and were preparing to move. We were also expecting a baby early July so "moving" for me really meant sitting and pointing. I was in our bedroom and Kyndl was in another room sorting through and throwing away junk we had collected over the years when I heard him casually say,

Sjhira Ellzey

"Do you need this?" I poked my head into the hallway to see him holding a black 3-ring binder with my handwriting on the front that read, "Sjhira's Notebook." I think my heart stopped beating for a moment as my eyes grew twice their size.

That binder looked very familiar, but it had been a long time since I had seen it and I questioned what could be inside. As I took hold of it my insides felt like they were about to burst. With bated breath I opened the front cover to a page that read, "Author's Dedication: everything about this book was inspired by the Holy Spirit, therefore, my dedication goes to the Lord."

Words cannot describe my feelings of shock, disbelief, gratitude, and awe. After eight years, including 3 moves, the lost pages of a sacred moment in history found their way back into my hands. I thought about all those times I had hoped and prayed for a miracle only to feel like the entire plan had died. I remembered the feelings of despair; that I had let God down. At that moment there was a glorious resurrection in my heart as I realized the Lord's plan for this book to happen was not contingent on me.

Overwhelmed by the awesome power of God, I pulled that binder tightly to my chest, dropped my head and wept for a long time. At that moment my heart and soul understood what Job meant when he said, *"I know that you can do all things, and that no purpose of yours can be thwarted," (Job 42:2).*

The Holy Spirit spoke to me in 2007 about writing this book. Am I, or is anyone, able to thwart the plan of God? In December 2015 a family friend I had not seen in years approached me after my father's memorial service and prophetically spoke into my life. I don't remember what she said verbatim but in a nutshell it was, *one day I believe you are going to write a book.* I smiled through my tears as I was grieving the loss of my daddy, politely thanked her and didn't give it much thought beyond that moment.

Two years later, when the Lord resurrected this book idea, I remembered her words. It was a divine set-up! God sees everything and has full knowledge of what's to come. Not only was this book a divine set-up for me, it was for you as well! My whole life was about to change with the arrival of a baby, and after 8 years, the Lord chose that particular time to say, *hey, remember that book I told you to write? Well, now is the time!* From our perspective His timing can be quite hilarious. From His perspective, it is always perfect. You see, I was in the perfect position to realize there was no way I could do it without Him.

    When my son was born I did nothing for about 10 months. Once the Lord gave me peace about getting started I had to rely on the Holy Spirit for each phase. He broke it up into bite sized pieces, not giving me more than I could handle at a time. The baby's nap time, lunch breaks at work, and nighttime, after putting my son down for bed, all became my writing sessions. Every single time I picked up a pen to write, or turned the computer on, there was so much grace to be able to mentally focus. Sometimes I only had 20 minutes!

    Instead of being overwhelmed or stressed out, the Father's excitement spilled over onto me and our time working together was truly a delight. No time was wasted. Considering all the factors for this book to be, it was nothing short of a miracle.

A DIVINE VALENTINE

Valentine's Day was approaching and I wanted to do something special for the ladies that attended our weekly campus Bible studies. Up until a few days before, I still had no ideas and became increasingly dis-heartened by conversations I had. Many students expressed a true sadness or hatred at the mention of Valentine's Day because they had no Valentine.

Later it was uncovered that the source of these feelings were far deeper than the absence of a Valentine, a.k.a., a boyfriend, but my continued thought was, *Jesus can be your Valentine!* Sounds cheesy, I know, which is why I never said those words out loud. The last thing these young women needed was a cheesy one-liner to try and lift their spirits.

I decided to ask God what He wanted to say to them. What message did He have for their hearts? All of a sudden I had a brilliant idea! God would give me a message in the form of a love letter, I would type it up, make a bunch of copies, and hand it out as a valentine from the Lord. Yes! I was so excited at this thought until the Holy Spirit spoke, causing my excitement to come to a screeching halt, *"No Sjhira, this is not going to be a generic letter. I have something personal to say to each woman; individual love notes."*

In all honesty my mind's response was similar to that of a non-compliant teenager with an attitude. *What? Individual love notes? Am I hearing this correctly? Lord, that's a lot of work!*

Between the two campuses we had anywhere from 25-40 ladies attending each week. I didn't understand how this was going to work being so close to the actual day, not to mention how awkward it would be to write *personalized* love letters to women and say, "these are actually from Jesus." Would they believe me? Would they feel as uncomfortable as I was feeling? Knowing my inner struggle, the Holy Spirit spoke again saying, *"Sjhira, I am going to share my heart with you like you asked. If you will be obedient and write down what I tell you, you will be amazed at what I am going to do. Do you trust me?"*

Peace flooded my entire being as I chose obedience, still not knowing how it would all play out. But the Lord captured my attention and my initial shock with an attitude turned into a holy reverence with deep intrigue. The evening of February 11, 2007, I sat on my couch with notebook paper, a pencil, and a very curious yet open heart.

"Ok Lord, here we go. I'm listening."

By the power of the Holy Spirit, I began hearing the heart of God in the form of love notes; some were as if a man were writing to his beloved, others sounded like a doting father writing to his little princess. When He spoke I could decipher between the end of one and the beginning of another. Each note was unique and very personal. He spoke with such passion. At times it was a romantic whisper and other times it was as if He was standing on top of a mountain declaring His love for the world to hear. Sometimes He laughed with joy or gave an endearing chuckle and other times it seemed He had difficulty getting the words out.

I often wrote, "..." to illustrate His many pauses in the middle of phrases. Several notes were accompanied with an incredible vision. I found myself absolutely mesmerized by what I was hearing and seeing. Experiencing the Father's heart in this way prompted fits of girly giggles, caused my jaw to drop, brought lots of tears, and even caused moments of blushing. And then there were times when the only appropriate response I could give was to drop to my knees in worship.

Ephesians 3:17-19 became very real to me that night. *Then Christ will make his home in your hearts as you trust in him. Your roots will grow down into God's love and keep you strong. And may you have the power to understand, as all God's people should, how wide, how long, how high, and how deep his love is. May you experience the love of Christ, though it is too great to understand fully. Then you will be made complete with all the fullness of life and power that comes from God (NLT).*

Sjhira Ellzey

The Holy Spirit also allowed me to know that He had a specific woman in mind as He spoke each note, and that it wasn't for me to try and figure it out. In fact, the Lord made it abundantly clear that I was to conceal the notes and let the students blindly pick one in no particular order. This ended up proving that the love notes were indeed from God himself with no help from me.

As a campus minister, I had been building relationships with many of these women and had knowledge of personal information. His instructions removed my fear of being viewed as disingenuous. Having said that, I did hear the Lord speak one name to me after writing one of the notes. It was the only name I heard that night. As I reread the words I realized how perfect it would be for that particular lady. It was so perfect I wanted to hand it to her directly and say with confidence, "I know this note is for you, God told me!" But the Lord reminded me of His specific instructions and then called me out, *"Sjhira, do you believe that if I want her to have this specific note I can get it in her hands with no help from you? Do you trust me?"*

Do you notice a theme here? **Trust.** The Lord continually reminded me of this simple yet difficult concept for our human flesh. When we walk with the Lord, living out His will for our lives, it will always require trust. My anticipation was now growing to an all-time high.

Once again, I agreed to remain obedient and continued to write until He told me to stop. I put my pencil down and counted 36 love notes! Next, I typed them, printed them, cut them in heart shapes and sealed each one in a brown paper bag. Mission accomplished! Well, not quite. The first part was done, and now I had to actually take them to our Bible studies and let the students pick one. As I looked at the sea of brown lunch bags covering my living room floor, even with all the crazy thoughts running through my head, I knew there was no turning back. A huge smile brightened my face as I thought about all the young ladies who were unknowingly about to receive a divine Valentine!

PERSPECTIVE SHIFT

Before we continue, let's have some fun! Imagine this: you're sitting by the fireplace at a local coffee shop, bundled up in a cozy sweater and sipping your favorite drink. It has been a long busy week and you finally have a moment to zone out. Naturally, you begin to people watch. To the right, you notice a middle aged Black man in a suit typing vigorously at his laptop and periodically loosening the knot in his tie. He seems slightly stressed but confident; possibly working on a business project that has a deadline quickly approaching.

To your left is a young lady, early 20's, lounging on a large comfy chair; legs tossed over one side-arm and a messy bun full of frizzy strawberry-blonde curls propped up on the other side. She has a fashion magazine in one hand and a coffee in the other. One of the pages has caught your eye because there is a super cute suede jacket that you immediately start creating an outfit for.

Your blank stare notices movement at the front door and your attention is diverted to an interracial couple; a Chinese man and a White woman, who enter in and walk to the counter. At first you question the relationship because the age lines on the woman's face put her about 15 years ahead of the man, but after watching them for a minute, you realize they must be on a date. Everything about their body language shouts nervous energy. Her ankles are crossed and she is clinging to her purse strap as if someone might try to grab it and run. The man wipes his hands on the sides of his coat and then fumbles for his wallet in his back pocket. Neither of them are talking much. You assume they found each other on a dating site and this is their first meet-up. You give them about 20 minutes of awkward chatter until the woman confesses that this just isn't going to work.

Chuckling softly to yourself, your silly thoughts are interrupted by a man's voice.

"May I sit here?"

Without thinking you politely respond, "Sure."

As your body shifts from a relaxed slouch to a more upright position, you nonchalantly glance around the room noticing there are several open seats and wonder why this stranger chose the one so uncomfortably close to you. Your personal space has been invaded and you are annoyed because your lazy afternoon of people watching has just come to an end.

As you gather your things the man smiles at you and without hesitation strikes up a very light-hearted, friendly conversation. Surprisingly, the conversation goes back and forth with ease and you find yourself sinking back into the comforts of your chair. There is no rhyme or reason to the flow of the discussion; it just continues smoothly and you are amused. Before you know it, you have completely lost track of time. It feels like you have been talking to a close friend reminiscing on precious memories or sharing current thoughts about life.

You feel relaxed and free to be yourself with no hidden criticism and no need to impress. At one point you realize that every time you speak he gives you his undivided attention as if you are the only one in the room. His eyes are not shifting to the door, his phone, or the menu of specialty drinks. Everything about his body language and unadulterated gaze gives you full confidence in knowing you are being heard. When he speaks you are intrigued by his lack of inhibitions. His gentle tone, quirky personality, and sense of humor are refreshing. You find that you thoroughly enjoy being in his presence. The conversation leaves you feeling charged, appreciated, secure, and peaceful. You are now delighted that this strange man chose to sit next to you.

Who is he? You might be thinking, umm, he's perfect and therefore doesn't exist. I don't blame you on that one! Can you picture this man being Jesus? If you were already thinking that, great! If not, it's time for a perspective shift! Go back and re-read the coffee shop scenario and picture the Lord God, Creator of all, as the man talking to you.

Unfortunately, many women have a difficult time imagining that scenario. After all, God is sitting on His big throne in Heaven watching the whole world. Surely there are more important matters that He needs to focus on; war, global hunger, the church revival with thousands of attendees, or even the heinous business of sex-trafficking. Why in the world would God sit with me and get lost in conversation?

The nerves of my upcoming final exam, frustrations of dating, or my feelings of disconnect amongst my peers are hardly important enough to hold His attention. Or maybe your thoughts go in a different direction. *If the Lord has anything to say to me I don't want to hear it. My image of God is a very large finger stretching down from the sky, wagging at me about the do's and don'ts of Christianity, with several booms of a thunderous voice that says, "Thou shalt repent sinner!"*

The truth is, you can't fathom how strong the desire is for God to communicate with you. And when He speaks to a soft, open heart, it will be awakened, not repelled. Psalm 139:17-18 says, His thoughts about you outnumber the grains of sand.

"How precious are your thoughts about me, O God. They cannot be numbered! I can't even count them; they outnumber the grains of sand!" (NLT)

Have you ever sat on a beach or in a sandbox and tried to count the grains of sand? I have, it's ridiculously impossible!

The Holy Spirit wanted me to share the coffee shop scenario because He knows that He has been misrepresented to many of His beloved daughters. Poor father (and mother) figures, any kind of abuse, religious church fluff, and the subtle manipulation of Satan, are among the many factors that hinder our closeness to the Lord. When you view King Jesus through cloudy lenses you will not be able to experience Him in the fullness that He desires. When you don't see Jesus clearly you are unable to see God, the Father, clearly because Jesus said He is the direct reflection of His Father.

"Whoever has seen me has seen the Father. How can you say, 'Show us the Father?' Do you not

believe that I am in the Father and the Father is in me?" (John 14:9-10).

    But there is good news! The Lord is merciful and is able to meet you right where you are. He alone is able to clear the fog so that you can move forward in fellowship with Him. I believe He is preparing you right now and your perspective is being shifted.

    There is an outpouring of the Father's heart in this book and He doesn't want you to miss it. The Lord wants you to soak Him up so that He overflows out of you.

    You see, we are not just here to live a comfortable life so that after 70-90 years we can look back and take pride in having achieved the "American Dream." As followers of Jesus, we are called to live for Him and with Him so that others may know Him. It's not about us, it's about Him. That means, when He says go, we go. When He says sit, we sit. When He says write, we write. And we do it, not because we are puppets connected to the strings of a master puppeteer, we do it because He has so captivated our hearts that we can't imagine living life any other way. In fact, life really begins by saying, "yes" to Jesus as Lord and Savior.

What lens have you been looking through? In what way is your perspective being shifted? Perhaps you are reading this book and are ready to admit that you have never surrendered your heart to Jesus. Living in a Christian home and going to church every Sunday does not mean you are automatically saved from eternal separation from God, which is death.

For all have sinned and fall short of the glory of God (Romans 3:23).

For the wages of sin is death, but the free gift of God is eternal life in Christ Jesus our Lord (Romans 6:23).

There has to be repentance and a re-birth into His Kingdom; that alone is your decision to make. If I'm speaking to you, now is your opportunity! I have included a simple prayer for you to pray to the Father.

Please understand that using the exact wording is not the point, it's about the posture of your heart, like the criminal on the cross in Luke 23:39-43.

> Prayer of Salvation:
>
> *Heavenly Father, I need you. I'm sorry for my sin that has separated us. I believe Jesus died on the cross for my sins and then rose from the dead in victory over the power of sin and death. You are the only one who was able to be a perfect sacrifice on my behalf. Father God, I receive the blood of Jesus as my atonement. Now Lord, I lay my life down at your feet and place my heart in your hands. I invite you into every area of my being—nothing is hidden anymore. Use me for your glory. In Jesus' name, Amen.*

Now imagine a multitude that you cannot count, including angels, and the Lord God himself, celebrating your new life in Jesus! This moment is not taken lightly. You have been "born-again," and now when the Heavenly Father looks at you He no longer sees your sin but the precious blood of Jesus. You will NEVER be the same! Please share this decision with someone you know who loves Jesus and get connected to a community of believers. This part of your walk with the Lord is vital. You were never meant to be alone in your faith.

> *"Just so, I tell you, there will be more joy in heaven over one sinner who repents than over ninety-nine righteous persons who need no repentance"*
> *(Luke 15:7).*

For those of you who have already given your life to the Lord but struggle with hearing His voice and feel bored or complacent, I have included a prayer for you. Again, you can pray what is written below or in your own words that come from the heart.

> Lord Jesus, I want to know You more. Open the eyes of my heart so that I can see You. Open the ears of my heart so that I can hear

You. I believe that You want to speak directly to me. Your word says, *"You will seek me and find me, when you seek me with all your heart" (Jeremiah 29:13).* So Lord, here I am. My heart is open and my heart is Yours. Show Yourself to me and saturate me with the outpouring of Your love. I choose to believe and trust You. In the name of Jesus, Amen.

Your perspective is now shifting to align with the perspective of Heaven. God is moving in your midst in the most beautiful and powerful ways. You have been born for such a time as this; to be an arrow of light that slices through the darkness. The Lord God breathed purpose inside of you and He has given you a voice. Now is the time to walk and speak confidently as a daughter of the Most-High God!

HEARING BY FAITH & DRENCHED BY LOVE

"How do you hear God's voice, and when you do, how do you know it's really Him?"

This is a common question I've heard over the years, especially when I was a campus minister. My short answer would be, when you get to know someone you can easily distinguish the sound of their voice. Going a step farther, knowing someone also means being able to discern their character. Once that happens, you can even anticipate a person's words and actions. If someone told me that my husband accidentally hit a dog with his car and then shrugged his shoulders as if it was no big deal, I would know they were lying. Why? Because I know my husband. He has a deep love for animals, especially dogs. It would be totally out of character for him to react that way. On a basic level, hearing and discerning the voice of God is no different.

Thankfully the Lord wants us to hear Him and He doesn't make it difficult, however, it will require discipline. My two biggest pieces of advice for a believer would be: slow down and read His Word. We tend to keep ourselves busy doing nothing; how many times do we need to check Instagram or some other form of social media within a 10-min timeframe? Some of you just need to turn the TV off. Be still, be quiet, and read your Bible.

I would encourage anyone to start with the gospels. Reading Jesus' own words and hearing about His time on earth, is a great way to get to know Him. Regardless of where in the Bible you are reading, interwoven throughout scripture is the character and voice of God. And remember, as a child of God, born-again, you have been given His Spirit to dwell in you, therefore, you have direct access to Him. Many people read the Bible and gain intellectual knowledge of God but sadly never get to know Him intimately. Let the Word of God renew your mind and trust the power of the Holy Spirit.

Now that you are familiarizing yourself with your Lord, you need to exercise faith. For example, when you read the story of Jesus visiting Mary and Martha (Luke 10:38-42), put yourself in the story. When Jesus talks to Martha, read it as if He is talking to you. Picture the Lord sitting on your couch next to you while you read His Word. If you have questions, ask Him for clarification. Talk to Him and believe that He is right there listening to you. Faith is a beautiful thing and pleases the Lord's heart. Those who believe Jesus by pure faith are surely blessed. In fact, that's what Jesus told Thomas after the resurrection.

So the disciples informed him, "We have seen the Lord with our own eyes!"

Still unconvinced, Thomas replied, "There's no way I'm going to believe this unless I personally see the wounds of the nails in his hands, touch them with my finger, and put my hand into the wound of his side where he was pierced!"

Then eight days later, Thomas and all the others were in the house together. And even though all the doors were locked, Jesus suddenly stood before them. *"Peace to you,"* he said. Then, looking into Thomas' eyes, he said, *"Put your finger here in the wounds of my hands. Here, put your hand into my wounded side and see for yourself. Thomas, don't give in to your doubts any longer, just believe!"*

Then the words spilled out of his heart, "You are my Lord, and You are my God!"

Jesus responded, *"Thomas, now that you've seen me, you believe. But there are those who have never seen me with their eyes but have believed in me with their hearts, and they will be blessed even more!"* (John 20:25-29 TPT).

Having said that, the Bible is filled with stories of how the Lord God revealed Himself to people in remarkable ways – the most powerful example, of course, would be Jesus coming to earth as a man. So, it is apparent that the Lord allows us to experience Him beyond just believing. Throughout my life I have had many God-encounters that were out of the ordinary from the day-to-day relationship we share. The word "amazing" just doesn't do them justice. The Lord always has a purpose in revealing Himself to me in these extraordinary ways. One in particular was a time when He drenched me with his love. Interestingly enough this happened on July 7, 2007, just 5 months after the students received their love notes.

This story actually began a month earlier when I was in Auckland, New Zealand for a friend's wedding. One morning I decided to go for a walk; enjoying the sunshine and the surroundings of a beautiful new country. At first, I was talking to the Lord like I usually do. Then, I began singing to Him. I heard the Lord say to me, *"Sjhira, I love when you sing to me. Your voice is beautiful and it fills my heart with such joy. Now, I want you to stop and listen because I want to sing to you."*

And then with a great big smile on my face I heard the Holy Spirit sing His love for me. At one point my hand was on my heart because it felt like my chest was going to explode with joy. As wonderful, precious, and real that time was, it didn't take long for the thought to pop up in my head, *Is He really singing*

Sjhira Ellzey

to you or is that your imagination? I brushed it off and thought, *well I'm pretty silly and I do have a great imagination so if it was just me making it up, it sure was awesome.*

A few days later I was invited to co-lead a small group Bible study at Auckland University with about 5 students. The campus minister leading the group was also a part of the same worldwide ministry I was a part of and we had met before at a conference. We started off with an icebreaker; taking a moment to write down the first word or bible verse that came to mind for each person in the group. Then we went around the circle and took turns sharing our words/verses. One of the students, I had never met before, looked at me and said, "Zephaniah 3:17."

The Lord your God is with you, the Mighty Warrior who saves. He will take great delight in you; in his love he will no longer rebuke you, but will rejoice over you with singing (NIV).

Then she briefly said that she heard music when looking at me and believed that the Lord delighted in singing over me. The voice I heard during my walk, that questioned if God really sang to me, was completely silenced. My heart was deeply moved and I thanked Jesus for the confirmation.

Fast forward a month later to July 7, 2007. I was back in Nashville, TN and attended "The Call," which was a time of worship to Jesus and prayer and fasting for America. The gathering took place in the Titans Football Stadium with over 70,000 people in attendance. Periodically, leaders would announce that there were 3 prayer tents available: a prophetic tent, a healing tent, and a Father's blessing tent. Each tent had ministers waiting to pray for people.

It was very hot that day and I stayed for many hours. When I decided to leave another announcement was made about the tents with a brief description on each one. The Father's blessing was for those who may not have had a good natural father example and needed an encouraging word from the Heavenly Father. The Holy Spirit told me to go to the Father's blessing tent.

Sjhira Ellzey

I was tired from fasting, hot from the sun, and ready to go. Admittedly, I was also not wanting anyone I knew to see me standing in line at that particular tent because I felt embarrassed. My pride was trying to convince me that it would look spiritually "weak" for me, a campus missionary, to need a "Father's blessing." And although my natural father wasn't the best Godly example in my life, he was present and certainly wasn't that bad. So, I argued with the Lord and said I knew I was blessed and didn't need to hear it through another person. The Holy Spirit, knowing the depths of my thoughts, simply said, *"You don't have to go but I have something I want to say to you."* I conceded and stood in a long line, for a long time in the hot sun, waiting for my turn to be blessed.

When it was my turn a middle-aged couple smiled and reached out their hands to greet me. There were tons of people under the tent, packed like sardines, with a lot of ministry team members praying. I stepped in closer so that we could hear each other. Once the names were exchanged, the man paused in silence and gave me a look that was a bit awkward. His wife gave him that, "honey, would you say something," look. I just stood there knowing there was no way out and waited for the awkward moment to pass.

The man finally spoke up, almost reluctantly, and apologized because he knew his behavior was strange. He then said, "I just have this overwhelming sense from the Father that He wants to sing to you. I've never done this before but instead of speaking the Father's blessing over you, the Lord wants me to sing it… and I'm not a singer, so, please bear with me."

Completely undone, my head dropped and I began to ugly-face sob as a complete stranger sang the same song the Holy Spirit sang to me a month prior while on my walk in New Zealand. Not only that, there was more to the song that I was able to hear and receive because the questioning voice was silent. That doubting voice in New Zealand was an interruption and the Father wanted to finish his song to me!

What can I even say. It's January 18, 2020, at 12:49 am, and tears are flowing down my cheeks as I write this story, recalling that moment when Jesus drenched me with His love. I share this God-encounter with you because I know with every cell in my body that He also desires to drench you with His love! Beloved sister in Christ, prepare to be embraced by the One True Living God. The same God that told me He wanted to sing to me over 10 years ago is thinking about you right now. He is the same God that looked into Thomas' eyes and told him to touch his wounded side. He is the same God who promised to come back for His beloved bride. He is real. He is alive. He is available and He is so in love with you!

Would you please do something? Go before the Lord and let Him have your doubts, your fears, your skepticism, and all your questions. Just lay it all at His feet. Stand before Him totally bare and naked and allow Him to cover you, cleanse you, and clothe you. You see, faith is saying, "Lord I believe and know, even if I don't see or fully understand. I believe You are there for me and Your affection is there for me even though I may not feel You." That kind of faith triggers the movement in God's Kingdom to directly impact your life! So, by faith, hear the Lord's voice as you read His Heart Expressions from the Throne Room.

Are you hungry? The appetizer was just the beginning. You now know why this book was written; it was written for you. Your perspective has shifted, your faith has strengthened, and your heart is ready to receive. It is now time for you to move on to the main course!

Part II
The Main Course

Heart Expressions from the Throne Room

When your words came, I ate them; they were my joy and my heart's delight, for I bear your name, Lord God Almighty (Jeremiah 15:16 NIV).

Heart Expressions from the Throne Room

When you read these heart expressions I strongly recommend you listen intently to what the Lord wants to say to you. Have your Bible with you and a pen. You may even want more paper to write on in addition to the blank space provided. For each love note I included scripture for you to consider, but you don't have to stop there. The Holy Spirit may lead you to another verse, or verses, that I did not write.

After reading these love notes over and over again, I am aware that some may take you by surprise or even cause you to question if God would really say *that*. Write down your honest feelings and thoughts. First and foremost, take your questions to the Lord and ask Him to clarify and confirm. Seek out wise counsel from a spiritual mentor that loves Jesus, and whom you trust.

Over the course of writing this book many prayers have gone forth by me and others. So, with confidence, I encourage you to receive the outpouring of His love. Again, don't rush; eating too fast isn't good for you! Take time and enjoy these moments with Jesus. Eat, drink, and be satisfied.

~I Will Wait for You~

I will wait for you my darling. I will wait patiently for your heart. You have been rushed before, criticized, ridiculed; I say, no more! Your heart is sensitive and delicate. As the reflection of a true gentlemen, I will wait patiently for you…patiently for your heart.

Scripture

The Lord does not delay and is not tardy or slow about what He promises, according to some people's conception of slowness, but He is long-suffering (extraordinarily patient) toward you, not desiring that any should perish, but that all should turn to repentance (2 Peter 3:9 AMPC).

Love is patient and kind; love does not envy or boast; it is not arrogant or rude. It does not insist on its own way; it is not irritable or resentful; it does not rejoice at wrongdoing, but rejoices with the truth. Love bears all things, believes all things, hopes all things, endures all things (1 Corinthians 13:4-7).

Sjhira Ellzey

Personal Reflection

Heart Expressions from the Throne Room

Sjhira Ellzey

~Hour, Minutes, and Seconds~

How many hours, minutes, seconds will pass before we are together again? Too many, for I desire to be with you at all times. Not a moment passes by without you on my mind. You are dearly loved by my heart.

Scripture

But do not overlook this one fact, beloved, that with the Lord one day is as a thousand years, and a thousand years as one day (2 Peter 3:8)

As the Father has loved me, so have I loved you. Abide in my love (John 15:9).

Personal Reflection

_____
_____
_____
_____
_____

Sjhira Ellzey

Heart Expressions from the Throne Room

~Precious Thoughts~

My love, your thoughts are precious to me. Your desires, so sincere, bless the heart of your king. My desire is to flood your soul with my love, removing every scar. Let me love you like no other. Allow me to present your desires to you one by one in a way that will leave you helplessly in love with me.

Scripture

And this hope is not a disappointing fantasy, because we can now experience the endless love of God cascading into our hearts through the Holy Spirit who lives in us (Romans 5:5 TPT).

Delight yourself in the Lord and he will give you the desires of your heart (Psalm 37:4).

Personal Reflection

_____

_____

Heart Expressions from the Throne Room

Sjhira Ellzey

~Magnificent Beauty~

Magnificent Beauty...not just pleasing to the eye, pleasing to the soul. I am the true lover of your soul and I am deeply pleased with you.

Scripture

This is the book of the generations of Adam. When God created man, he made him in the likeness of God (Genesis 5:1).

But the Lord said to Samuel, "Do not look on his appearance or on the height of his stature, because I have rejected him. For the Lord sees not as man sees: man looks on the outward appearance, but the Lord looks on the heart (1 Samuel 16:7).

And without faith it is impossible to please God, because anyone who comes to him must believe that he exists and that he rewards those who earnestly seek him (Hebrews 11:6 NIV).

Sjhira Ellzey

Personal Reflection

Heart Expressions from the Throne Room

Sjhira Ellzey

~My Heart at Rest~

Beauty that leaves my heart at rest; never needing to gaze upon another for satisfaction. Those are my thoughts when I look at your sweet face.

Scripture

God said, Let Us [Father, Son, and Holy Spirit] make mankind in Our image after Our likeness, and let them have complete authority over the fish of the sea, the birds of the air, the [tame] beasts, and over all the earth and over everything that creeps upon the earth. So God created man in His own image, in the image and likeness of God He created him; male and female He created them (Genesis 1:26,27 AMPC).

Gaze upon him, join your life with his, and joy will come. Your faces will glisten with glory. You'll never wear that shame-face again (Psalm 34:5 TPT).

For your royal Bridegroom is ravished by your beautiful brightness. Bow in reverence before him, for he is your Lord! (Psalm 45:11 TPT).

Personal Reflection

_____
_____
_____
_____
_____
_____
_____
_____
_____
_____
_____
_____
_____
_____

Heart Expressions from the Throne Room

Sjhira Ellzey

~When You Said, "Yes"~

My dearest beloved, when you said "yes" my heart rejoiced! What could you possibly do to make me stop loving you? What could you say that would stop my heart from beating the syllables of your name? What could you think that would cause me to not be constantly mindful of you? Nothing...and I repeat nothing!

<u>Scripture</u>

Then, by constantly using your faith, the life of Christ will be released deep inside you, and the resting place of his love will become the very source and root of your life. Then you will be empowered to discover what every holy one experiences – the great magnitude of the astonishing love of Christ in all its dimensions. How deeply intimate and far-reaching is his love! How enduring and inclusive it is! Endless love beyond measurement that transcends our understanding – this extravagant love pours into you until you are filled to overflowing with the fullness of God! (Ephesians 3:17-19 TPT).

Come out and look, you daughters of Zion. Look on King Solomon wearing a crown, the crown with which his mother crowned him on the day of his wedding, the day his heart rejoiced (Song of Songs 3:11 NIV)

Every single moment you are thinking of me! How precious and wonderful to consider that you cherish me constantly in your every thought! (Psalm 139:17 TPT).

Personal Reflection

_____
_____
_____
_____
_____
_____
_____
_____

Heart Expressions from the Throne Room

Sjhira Ellzey

~Love-Sick~

Dearest beloved, I become love-sick at the thought of not spending eternity with you. Let us run away and hide in a secret place, just me and you. I alone will protect you. I alone will sustain you. I alone will give you everything you need and so much more. Come with me to the secret place and be mine forever!

Scripture
For in the day of trouble He will hide me in His shelter; in the secret place of His tent will He hide me; He will set me high upon a rock (Psalm 27:5 AMPC).

My lover said to me, Rise up, my darling! Come away with me, my fair one...Rise up, my darling! Come away with me, my fair one! (Song of Songs 2:10,13 NLT).

There was such a swirl of activity around Jesus, with so many people coming and going, that they were unable to even eat a meal. So Jesus said to his disciples, "Come, let's take a break and find a secluded place where you can rest a while," (Mark 6:31 TPT).

He who dwells in the secret place of the Most High shall abide under the shadow of the Almighty (Psalm 91:1 NKJV)

Personal Reflection

_____
_____
_____
_____
_____
_____
_____
_____
_____
_____

Heart Expressions from the Throne Room

Sjhira Ellzey

~Rose Petals~

A bed of rose petals – not enough. A sweet kiss under the Tuscan sun – not good enough. A love song written just for you and sung softly in your ear as you drift asleep...it's just not good enough. You, my love, shall be romanced beyond what the things of this world can offer and I will be the one to romance you.

Scripture
Now to Him who is able to do exceedingly abundantly above all that we ask or think, according to the power that works in us, to Him be glory in the church by Christ Jesus to all generations, forever and ever. Amen (Ephesians 3:20-21).

Eye has not seen, nor ear heard, nor have entered into the heart of man the things which God has prepared for those who love Him. But God has revealed them to us through His Spirit. For the Spirit searches all things, yes, the deep things of God (1 Corinthians 2:9-10 NKJV).

...because we don't focus our attention on what is seen but on what is unseen. For what is seen is temporary, but the unseen realm is eternal (2 Corinthians 4:18 TPT).

<u>Personal Reflection</u>

_____
_____
_____
_____
_____
_____
_____
_____
_____
_____
_____
_____

Heart Expressions from the Throne Room

Sjhira Ellzey

~Joy~

There is a joy in my heart that I cannot fully explain. It causes my heart to leap, my lips to smile, my soul to sing and my feet to dance. Joy that causes my sorrow to be forgotten and my tears to be no more. This joy goes so deep that nothing will ever be able to take it away. Do you know the source of this joy? Beloved, it is none other than you!

Scripture

The Lord your God is in your midst, a mighty one who will save; he will rejoice over you with gladness; he will quiet you by his love; he will exult over you with loud singing (Zephaniah 3:17).

We look away from the natural realm and we fasten our gaze onto Jesus who birthed faith within us and who leads us forward into faith's perfection. His example is this: because his heart was focused on the joy of knowing that you would be his, he endured the agony of the cross and conquered its humiliation, and now sits exalted at the right hand of the throne of God! (Hebrews 12:2 TPT).

Personal Reflection

Heart Expressions from the Throne Room

Sjhira Ellzey

~Close to You~

Just to be close to you is what my heart wants.
Just to be close to you is my one desire.
Just to be close to you is my true delight.
When I am close to you, you take my breath away. I would give my life again...just to be close to you.

Scripture

The word became flesh and made his dwelling among us. We have seen his glory, the glory of the one and only Son, who came from the Father, full of grace and truth (John 1:14 NIV).

But now you have been united with Christ Jesus. Once you were far away from God, but now you have been brought near to him through the blood of Christ (Ephesians 2:13 NLT).

The Lord is close to all who call on him, yes, to all who call on him in truth (Psalm 145:18 NLT).

Come close to God, and God will come close to you. Wash your hands, you sinners; purify your hearts, for your loyalty is divided between God and the world (James 4:8 NLT).

Personal Reflection
___

Heart Expressions from the Throne Room

Sjhira Ellzey

Heart Expressions from the Throne Room

~One True Love~

You are my one true love. You fill my heart in a way that no one else can. There is a deep void without you. I yearn for you.
I long for you. I want you and I need you.
I want all of you, the good and the bad.
Nothing else will do...I want you!

Scripture

However, those the Father has given me will come to me, and I will never reject them (John 6:37 NLT).

But God showed his great love for us by sending Christ to die for us while we were still sinners (Romans 5:8 NLT).

Does the Scripture mean nothing to you that says, "The Spirit that God breathed into our hearts is a jealous Lover who intensely desires to have more and more of us" (James 4:5 TPT)?

Personal Reflection

Heart Expressions from the Throne Room

Sjhira Ellzey

~Form and Feature~

*What a beautiful young woman you are. Perfect in form and feature. I look at you in awe. How lovely you are to me – every part of you.
Let not a man define your beauty but the very words spoken from my heart.*

Scripture

So God created man in His own image; in the image of God He created him; male and female He created them. Then God saw everything that He had made, and indeed it was very good…(Genesis 1:27, 31 NKJV)

You made all the delicate, inner parts of my body and knit me together in my mother's womb. Thank you for making me so wonderfully complex! Your workmanship is marvelous – how well I know it (Psalm 139:13-14 NLT).

You are altogether beautiful, my love; there is no flaw in you (Song of Songs 4:7).

Personal Reflection

Heart Expressions from the Throne Room

Sjhira Ellzey

~I Am Near~

Beloved, I am near. Though I seem far at times,
I am closer than you often realize.
I will never leave you, never reject you,
never abandon you.
I will stay close by your side.
You can be sure of that.

Scripture

So be strong and courageous!...For the Lord your God will personally go ahead of you. He will neither fail you nor abandon you (Deuteronomy 31:6 NLT).

Seek the Lord while he may be found; call upon him while he is near (Isaiah 55:6).

Be strong and courageous. Do not be frightened, and do not be dismayed, for the Lord your God is with you wherever you go (Joshua 1:9).

Personal Reflection

Heart Expressions from the Throne Room

Sjhira Ellzey

~Lift Your Eyes~

Oh, the joy my heart experiences when you lift your eyes to my throne. The only way I can express this joy in its fullest measure is from heart to heart; my heart to yours. It is unique and I desire to share this joy with you alone!

Scripture

To you I lift up my eyes, O you who are enthroned in the heavens (Psalm 123:1).

In the same way, there is more joy in heaven over one lost sinner who repents and returns to God than over ninety-nine others who are righteous and haven't strayed away! (Luke 15:7 NLT).

Personal Reflection

_____
_____
_____
_____

Sjhira Ellzey

Heart Expressions from the Throne Room

Sjhira Ellzey

~Hidden Treasure~

You are my hidden treasure and I have the key
that unlocks your precious jewels.
No key shall be given to the unworthy.
I have the key and I alone will choose who is
worthy to partake of my
precious treasure – that is you.

Scripture

The kingdom of heaven is like treasure hidden in a field, which a man found and covered up. Then in his joy he goes and sells all that he has and buys that field (Matthew 13:44).

For where your treasure is, there your heart will be also (Matthew 6:21).

Where you deposit your treasure, that is where your thoughts will turn to – and your heart will long to be there also (Luke 12:34 TPT).

Heart Expressions from the Throne Room

Personal Reflection

Sjhira Ellzey

Heart Expressions from the Throne Room

Sjhira Ellzey

~Sweetness~

Sweetness, you are sweet to the touch, to the eye, and none compares to you. Sweeter than a summer's breeze, sweeter than a fragrance that makes a man weak in his knees. Sweeter than a field of wild-flowers or a bushel of roses. Sweetness that lingers and is enjoyed by all, but most importantly it is enjoyed by me.

<u>Scripture</u>

...show me your face, let me hear your voice; for your voice is sweet, and your face is lovely (Song of Songs 2:14 NIV).

God always makes his grace visible in Christ, who includes us as partners of his endless triumph. Through our yielded lives he spreads the fragrance of the knowledge of God everywhere we go (2 Corinthians 2:14 TPT).

# Heart Expressions from the Throne Room

Personal Reflection

Heart Expressions from the Throne Room

Sjhira Ellzey

~The Perfect Sunset~

The perfect sunset, the early sunrise, the radiant sparkle of a rainbow, the intensity of the blue Caribbean Sea, the most delicate flower petal, the fresh fragrance after the rain, the twinkle of a starry sky on a clear night, the brilliance of a perfectly cut diamond…my love, none of that even compares to you.

Scripture
Look at the birds. They don't plant or harvest or store food in barns, for your heavenly Father feeds them. And aren't you far more valuable to him than they are? (Matthew 6:26 NLT).

She is more precious than jewels, and nothing you desire can compare with her (Proverbs 3:15).

When I view and consider Your heavens, the work of Your fingers, the moon and the stars, which You have ordained and established, what is man that You are

Heart Expressions from the Throne Room

mindful of him, the son of [earthborn] man that You care for him? (Psalm 8:3-4 AMPC).

Personal Reflection

Sjhira Ellzey

Heart Expressions from the Throne Room

Sjhira Ellzey

~Speechless...Breathless~

My dear, when I made you I was speechless. Such an exquisite creation; delicately molded by my very hands. All of Heaven watched as I made you, it was a sight to behold and to this day you leave me breathless at the very thought of you.

Scripture

For you formed my inward parts; you knitted me together in my mother's womb. I praise you, for I am fearfully and wonderfully made. Wonderful are your works; my soul knows it very well. My frame was not hidden from you, when I was being made in secret, intricately woven in the depths of the earth (Psalm 139:13-15).

Before I formed you in the womb I knew you..., (Jeremiah 1:5).

Heart Expressions from the Throne Room

And Jesus uttered a loud cry and breathed his last (Mark 15:37).

Personal Reflection

Heart Expressions from the Throne Room

Sjhira Ellzey

~Knight in Shining Armor~

I want to be your knight in shining armor. I want to rescue you from a tower, like when a maiden waits for her prince, and he comes to take her away from all that is dangerous. Come with me and be my maiden, the one whom my heart adores. I have fought for you because your love was worth the fight. Just to have you in my arms once again was worth the fight.

Scripture
You must not fear them, for the Lord your God Himself fights for you (Deuteronomy 3:22 NKJV).

May God the Father and our Lord Jesus Christ give you grace and peace. Jesus gave his life for our sins, just as God our Father planned, in order to rescue us from this evil world in which we live (Galatians 1:3-4 NLT).

Those who live in the shelter of the Most High will find rest in the shadow of the Almighty. This I declare about the Lord: He alone is my refuge, my place of safety; he is my God, and I trust him. For he will rescue you from every trap and protect you from deadly disease. He will cover you with his feathers. He will shelter you with his wings. His faithful promises are your armor and protection...The Lord says, I will rescue those who love me. I will protect those who trust in my name. When they call on me, I will answer; I will be with them in trouble. I will rescue and honor them (Psalm 91:1-4,14-15 NLT).

Personal Reflection

_____

_____

_____

_____

_____

_____

_____

_____

_____

_____

Sjhira Ellzey

Heart Expressions from the Throne Room

~Awakened by Beauty~

My heart is awakened by your beauty at the rising sun. A smile forms on my lips as I see you awake from your slumber. There is no flaw in what my eyes see and my heart is falling deeper in love with you at each passing day.

Scripture

You are altogether beautiful, my love; there is no flaw in you...You have captivated my heart, my sister my bride; you have captivated my heart with one glance of your eyes...(Song of Songs 4:7,9).

Those who look to him are radiant, and their faces shall never be ashamed (Psalm 34:5).

Personal Reflection

_____
_____
_____
_____

Heart Expressions from the Throne Room

Sjhira Ellzey

~Just Me and You~

My love, I look forward to the moments when it is just me and you. We don't need anything or anyone else in order to experience the truest form of intimacy. My heart is content, my heart is full and my joy is complete with you by my side.

Scripture

So when that day comes, you will know that I am living in the Father and that you are one with me, for I will be living in you (John 14:20 TPT).

I have told you these things, that My joy and delight may be in you, and that your joy and gladness may be of full measure and complete and overflowing (John 15:11 AMPC).

Personal Reflection

_____

_____

Sjhira Ellzey

Heart Expressions from the Throne Room

~I Danced~

Ah yes, the day that you were born I danced. I danced...there was such joy in my heart I did not know what else to do. Will you dance with me my darling? It does not matter who is looking. I just want to dance with you and celebrate your glorious life!

Scripture

The Prodigal Son (Luke 15:11-32)

And kill the calf we have been fattening. We must celebrate with a feast, for this son of mine was dead and has now returned to life. He was lost, but now he is found. So the party began. Meanwhile, the older son was in the fields working. When he returned home, he heard music and dancing in the house...We had to celebrate this happy day. For your brother was dead and has come back to life! He was lost, but now he is found! (Luke 15:23-25,32 NLT).

And David danced before the Lord with all his might (2 Samuel 6:14).

Then he broke through and transformed all my wailing into a whirling dance of ecstatic praise! He has torn the veil and lifted from me the sad heaviness of mourning. He wrapped me in the glory garments of gladness. How could I be silent when it's time to praise you? Now my heart sings out loud, bursting with joy- a bliss inside that keeps me singing, I can never thank you enough! (Psalm 30:11-12 TPT).

Personal Reflection

_____
_____
_____
_____
_____
_____
_____
_____

Sjhira Ellzey

Heart Expressions from the Throne Room

Sjhira Ellzey

~Softly Kiss You~

Oh won't you please allow me to hold your face gently in the palm of my hands and softly kiss you? A kiss of purity and wholeness that will leave your heart deeply satisfied; never again restless or disturbed. A kiss that brings freedom, not bondage. A kiss you will want to remember and never forget.

Scripture

Greet one another with a holy kiss (Romans 16:16/1 Corinthians 16:20).

He kisses the lips [and wins the hearts of men] who give a right answer (Proverbs 24:26).

Let him kiss me with the kisses of his mouth! For your love is better than wine (Song of Songs 1:2).

Personal Reflection

Heart Expressions from the Throne Room

Sjhira Ellzey

~Lovely~

Lovely, I see you and you are lovely. Every dream, every desire, every thought...I notice everything about you. Every smile, every tear, every burst of laughter, every move you make. You are lovely. I notice you and I want you to know that you are lovely.

Scripture

The Lord looks over us from where he rules in heaven. Gazing into every heart from his lofty dwelling place, he observes all the peoples of the earth. The Creator of our hearts considers and examines everything we do (Psalm 33:13-15 TPT).

For your royal Bridegroom is ravished by your beautiful brightness. Bow in reverence before him, for he is your Lord! (Psalm 45:11 TPT).

So don't worry. For your Father cared deeply about even the smallest detail of your life...But even the very hairs of your head are all numbered (Matthew 10:30 TPT...AMPC).

Personal Reflection

Heart Expressions from the Throne Room

Sjhira Ellzey

~Your Tears~

Your tears are beautiful to me. I have each one saved in a jar. I will never forget those times you cried. My precious one, I was there collecting your tears. I care when no one else cares. I'm present when everyone is gone. I listen when no one else listens. Tears are not forgotten, they are collected and you are restored.

Scripture

You've kept track of all my wandering and my weeping. You've stored my many tears in your bottle- not one will be lost (Psalm 56:8 TPT).

This is what the Lord, the God of your ancestor David, says: I have heard your prayer and seen your tears. I will heal you…(2 King 20:5 NLT).

He will wipe every tear from their eyes, and there will be no more death or sorrow or crying or pain. All these things are gone forever (Revelation 21:4 NLT).

Sjhira Ellzey

Personal Reflection

Heart Expressions from the Throne Room

Sjhira Ellzey

~For an Eternity~

*Do you know how special you are to me?
If I took a lifetime to explain that to you, time would run out and I would have just begun. That is why I have eternity with you on my heart. For an eternity I will show you how special you are to me...and
I will never be able to stop.*

Scripture

But do not overlook this one fact, beloved, that with the Lord one day is as a thousand years, and a thousand years as one day (2 Peter 3:8).

He has made everything beautiful in its time. He has also set eternity in the human heart; yet no one can fathom what God has done from beginning to end (Ecclesiastes 3:11 NIV).

This is why the scriptures say: Things never discovered or heard of before, things beyond our ability to imagine – these are the many things God has in store for all his lovers. But God now unveils these profound realities to us by the Spirit. Yes, he has revealed to us his inmost heart and deepest mysteries through the Holy Spirit, who constantly explores all things (1 Corinthians 2:9-10 TPT).

Personal Reflection

_____
_____
_____
_____
_____
_____
_____
_____
_____
_____
_____
_____

Heart Expressions from the Throne Room

Sjhira Ellzey

~Beautiful Bride~

I know your heart. I know your desire to be the most beautiful bride man has laid his eyes on. Well, my dear, I see your wedding day and I, your husband, think you are most beautiful indeed!

<u>Scripture</u>

For your Maker is your husband, the Lord of hosts is his name; and the Holy One of Israel is your Redeemer, the God of the whole earth he is called (Isaiah 54:5).

When that day comes, says the Lord, you will call me my husband instead of my master (Hosea 2:16 NLT).

All glorious is the princess in her chamber, with robes interwoven with gold. In many-colored robes she is led to the king, with her virgin companions following behind her (Psalm 45:13-14).

Sjhira Ellzey

<u>Personal Reflection</u>

Heart Expressions from the Throne Room

Sjhira Ellzey

Heart Expressions from the Throne Room

~Love Language~

There is no phrase in the human language eloquent enough to express my love for you. For this reason, I love you from my heart in a way that is unexplainable and leaves you speechless and in awe. In silence you will hear the whispers of my love language, specifically constructed for the secret places of your heart to understand.

Scripture

And I pray that he would unveil within you the unlimited riches of his glory and favor until supernatural strength floods your innermost being with his divine might and explosive power. Then, by constantly using your faith, the life of Christ will be released deep inside you, and the resting place of his love will become the very source and root of your life. Then you will be empowered to discover what every holy one experiences – the great magnitude of the astonishing love of Christ in all its dimensions. How deeply intimate and far-reaching is his love! How enduring and inclusive it is! Endless love beyond measurement that transcends our understanding – this extravagant love pours into you until you are filled to overflowing with the fullness of God! (Ephesians 3:16-19 TPT).

And rising very early in the morning, while it was still dark, he departed and went out to a desolate place, and there he prayed (Mark 1:35).

Be still, and know that I am God…(Psalm 46:10).

Personal Reflection

_____
_____
_____
_____
_____
_____
_____
_____

Heart Expressions from the Throne Room

Sjhira Ellzey

Heart Expressions from the Throne Room

~Elegance~

Elegance...the way you carry yourself, the way you walk and talk is elegant. You are a true woman in the perfect way I made you. You grace the world with your elegance, but most importantly you grace the heart of your king.

Scripture

Esther Chosen Queen (Esther 2:1-18)
The young woman had a beautiful figure and was lovely to look at...And the young woman pleased him and won his favor...the king loved Esther more than all the women, and she won grace and favor in his sight more than all the virgins, so that he set the royal crown on her head and made her queen instead of Vashti (Esther 2:7,9,17).

She is clothed with strength and dignity and she laughs without fear of the future...Charm is deceptive, and

beauty does not last; but a woman who fears the Lord will be greatly praised (Proverbs 31:25,30 NLT).
For your royal husband delights in your beauty; honor him, for he is your lord (Psalm 45:11 NLT).

Personal Reflection
_____
_____
_____
_____
_____
_____
_____
_____
_____
_____
_____
_____
_____
_____
_____

Heart Expressions from the Throne Room

Sjhira Ellzey

~Gaze in Wonder~

My love, I could never get bored or weary of just gazing at you. I gaze in wonder. I am intrigued. What in all the earth compares to your beauty? There is nothing. I could search for eternity and find nothing.

Scripture

Let the king be enthralled by your beauty; honor him, for he is your lord (Psalm 45:11 NIV).

She is more precious than jewels, and nothing you desire can compare with her (Proverbs 3:15).

Turn away your eyes from me, for they overwhelm me…(Song of Songs 6:5).

Personal Reflection

_____

_____

_____

Sjhira Ellzey

Heart Expressions from the Throne Room

Sjhira Ellzey

~Romanced~

You say you want to be loved? You say you want to be romanced and swept off your feet? Baby girl, I am love and the true lover of your soul. I created romance and placed the desire in your heart to be swept off your feet. No one can love you like I love you. I want to be the one who wins your heart. Dare to ask me and watch how I take your breath away.

Scripture

God showed how much he loved us by sending his one and only Son into the world so that we might have eternal life through him. This is real love – not that we loved God, but that he loved us and sent his Son as a sacrifice to take away our sins (1 John 4:9-10 NLT).

Therefore, behold, I will allure her [Israel] and bring her into the wilderness, and I will speak tenderly and to her heart (Hosea 2:14 AMPC).

Heart Expressions from the Throne Room

Ask, and it will be given to you; seek, and you will find; knock, and it will be opened to you. For everyone who asks receives, and the one who seeks finds, and to the one who knocks it will be opened (Matthew 7:7-8).

Personal Reflection

Sjhira Ellzey

Heart Expressions from the Throne Room

Sjhira Ellzey

~Together as One~

I long for the day when I will crown you as my bride. I will be your king and you will be my queen and eternity will be ours.
Together as one: nothing will stop us, come between us, or separate us.
Your crown is a seal – we are one.

Scripture

Fasten me upon your heart as a seal of fire forevermore. This living, consuming flame will seal you as my prisoner of love…(Song of Songs 8:6 TPT).

And when the Chief Shepherd appears, you will receive the unfading crown of glory (1 Peter 5:4).

And I am convinced that nothing can ever separate us from God's love. Neither death nor life, neither angels nor demons, neither our fears for today nor our worries about tomorrow – not even the powers of hell can separate us from God's love. No power in the sky above or in the earth below – indeed, nothing in all creation will ever be able to separate us from the love of God that is revealed in Christ Jesus our Lord (Romans 8:38-39 NLT).

Personal Reflection
___
___
___
___
___
___
___
___
___
___
___
___
___
___
___
___

Sjhira Ellzey

Heart Expressions from the Throne Room

Sjhira Ellzey

~I Will Carry You~

Sweetheart, you need not fight any longer. I am strong and my strength will be your strength. Come to me and I will gladly carry you. I will lift you up and bring you to safety. In my house you will rest and be satisfied.

Scripture

...this day is holy to our Lord. And do not be grieved, for the joy of the Lord is your strength (Nehemiah 8:10).

You shall not fear them, for it is the Lord your God who fights for you (Deuteronomy 3:22).

Then Jesus said, "Come to me, all of you who are weary and carry heavy burdens, and I will give you rest. Take my yoke upon you. Let me teach you, because I am humble and gentle at heart, and you will find rest for your souls. For my yoke is easy to bear, and the burden I give you is light," (Matthew 11:28-30 NLT).

Personal Reflection
___

Sjhira Ellzey

Heart Expressions from the Throne Room

Sjhira Ellzey

~Hold My Hand~

Hold my hand, draw close to me. Allow yourself to receive from me; my tender words, my loving gaze, my deep touch. Helplessly need me, desperately long for me. I will not fail you. My sweetheart, you will not be disappointed.

Scripture
For I, the Lord your God, hold your right hand; it is I who say to you, "Fear not, I am the one who helps you," (Isaiah 41:13).

Come to me with your ears wide open. Listen, and you will find life. I will make an everlasting covenant with you. I will give you all the unfailing love I promised to David...Seek the Lord while you can find him. Call on him now while he is near (Isaiah 55:3,6 NLT).

I long to drink of you, O God, drinking deeply from the streams of pleasure flowing from your presence. My longings overwhelm me for more of you! My soul

Heart Expressions from the Throne Room

thirsts, pants and longs for the living God. I want to come and see the face of God (Psalm 42:1-2 TPT).

Personal Reflection

Sjhira Ellzey

Heart Expressions from the Throne Room

Sjhira Ellzey

~Radiant~

You, my love, are radiant.
As a ray of light peeks through the clouds
and shines upon the earth, so does your soul
radiate through the dark places in this world
and touch the heart of man.

Scripture

You are the light of the world. A city set on a hill cannot be hidden. Nor do people light a lamp and put it under a basket, but on a stand, and it gives light to all in the house. In the same way, let your light shine before others, so that they may see your good works and give glory to your Father who is in heaven (Matthew 5:14-16).

Life came into being because of him, for his life is light for all humanity. And this Living Expression is the Light that bursts through gloom – the Light that darkness could not diminish! (John1:4-5 TPT).

Heart Expressions from the Throne Room

Commit everything you do to the Lord. Trust him, and he will help you. He will make your innocence radiate like the dawn, and the justice of your cause will shine like the noonday sun (Psalm 37:4-5 NLT).

Personal Reflection

Sjhira Ellzey

Heart Expressions from the Throne Room

Sjhira Ellzey

~Mystery to Behold~

A mystery to behold...when you walk away I follow. There is a part of me living inside of you and I cannot rest until we discover this truth together.

Scripture

And they heard the sound of the Lord God walking in the garden in the cool of the day, and the man and his wife hid themselves from the presence of the Lord God among the trees of the garden. But the Lord God called to the man and said to him, "Where are you?" (Genesis 3:8-9).

You go before me and follow me. You place your hand of blessing on my head. I can never escape from your Spirit! I can never get away from your presence! If I go up to heaven, you are there; if I go down to the grave, you are there. If I ride the wings of the morning, if I dwell by the farthest oceans, even there your hand will guide me and your strength will support me. I could ask the darkness to hide me and the light around me to become night – but even in darkness I cannot hide from you. To you the night shines as bright as day. Darkness and light are the same to you (Psalm 139:5,7-12 NLT).

If a man has a hundred sheep and one of them gets lost, what will he do? Won't he leave the ninety-nine others in the wilderness and go to search for the one that is lost until he finds it? And when he has found it, he will joyfully carry it home on his shoulders. When he arrives, he will call together his friends and neighbors saying, "Rejoice with me because I have found my lost sheep," (Luke 15:4-6 NLT).

<u>Personal Reflection</u>

_____
_____
_____
_____
_____
_____

Sjhira Ellzey

Heart Expressions from the Throne Room

Part III
The Dessert

Personal Stories from College Women

How sweet are your words to my taste, sweeter than honey to my mouth! (Psalm 119:103).

Have you left room for dessert? I hope so, because this next part is a real treat. In the following pages you will hear about the impact these heart expressions from the main course had on college women.

The first set of love notes were delivered the evening of February 13, 2007, at Fisk University. I randomly removed about half of the brown paper bags from my trunk and placed them on a round table in the meeting room. After a brief explanation, each lady chose a bag and read their love note. The remaining notes were taken to Tennessee State University the next evening, February 14, 2007, and again, after a brief explanation, the ladies chose a bag and read their personal message from the Lord.

Out of the 36 love notes written I was able to interview 28 women over the course of several weeks. As a way to honor and protect them I have changed all of their names. I spent many months with some of these ladies; building a relationship of trust, hearing personal information, and ministering to their hearts. These women are precious to me and I am eternally grateful that the Lord allowed our paths to cross.

Please understand that their stories are recorded without any fluff and I was very careful to include quotes accurately. Some students had a lot to say and others did not. Some were still processing the impact that was being made on their hearts. In many cases, I included my own commentary based on their responses and/or based on what the Holy Spirit was showing me. With deep joy in my heart, I present to you the stories of these lovely women. May the lover of our souls be glorified in and through them!

My love, your thoughts are precious to me. Your desires, so sincere, bless the heart of your king. My desire is to flood your soul with my love- removing every scar. Let me love you like no other. Allow me to present your desires to you one by one in a way that will leave you helplessly in love with me.

*

"*Just because you care about someone else, don't let that get in your way. Don't put that above God.*"
-Lauryn

*

During the fall semester Lauryn was dating a dude. In the beginning of their relationship they attended church and Bible study but then stopped. Lauryn admitted that she placed the desire for her boyfriend above the Lord and lost interest in having a relationship with God altogether. In fact, Lauryn did not receive her love note on Valentine's Day because she didn't show up to the campus Bible study until a month later. She received her love note March 9th and we spoke about it 5 days later on March 14th.

Three parts of the love note stood out. The first was, "Let me love you like no other." Considering the fact that Lauryn confessed she had made her boyfriend an idol in her life, this message from the Lord was very timely. Within minutes, she knew God was affirming His desire for her heart; her whole heart. He no longer wanted her to worship idols because He knew they would not satisfy her. Lauryn also mentioned how her love for parties and even friendships could not compare to God's love for her. She confessed, "He should always be first in my life. I should prioritize Him above all things."

The second part that stood out to her was, "I desire to flood your soul with my love, removing every scar." She interpreted the scars as doubts, worries, and anxieties. In Lauryn's words, "Everything I doubt or worry about I can just give to Him. He will take it away so I can just have love in my heart."

The third part was, "Let me present your desires to you one by one..." The Holy Spirit revealed to Lauryn the importance of patience. In the Lord's perfect timing He would present her desires in such a way that her heart would be drawn deeper into Him. A vision of Christmas Eve filled her mind as she pictured children who were eager to rip open their presents all at once. Instead, the Lord showed her how the "presents" would be given one by one and piece by piece, so that she knew they were from Him and she would give Him all the glory.

The Lord is gracious! Lauryn could have missed out completely on receiving this love note, but the Lord got it in her hands in His perfect timing. Showing up to our campus Bible study in March was Lauryn's response to a tug on her heart. The love note sparked a fresh new hunger for her Creator! She began reading her Bible again and a relationship with Jesus was once again her priority!

Sjhira Ellzey

Magnificent beauty...not just pleasing to the eye, pleasing to the soul. I am the true lover of your soul and I am deeply pleased with you.

*

"I believed that I wasn't worth God's grace and mercy."
-Tiffany

*

Four months before receiving her love note Tiffany attended our campus ministry's fall retreat. The second night of the retreat, Tiffany shared feelings of being overwhelmed by family, school, and personal issues. She was trying to be miss fix-it but felt like a failure. As tears streamed down her face, one of the campus staff looked at her and said, "God is pleased with you." There was a look of shock and disbelief on her face. Several staff, myself included, prayed for her and affirmed her by repeating that simple phrase, God is pleased with you. The Holy Spirit was at work in Tiffany's heart. That night she chose to believe the truth that was being spoken over her and she left the retreat refreshed and at rest.

In the months leading up to Valentine's Day, the battle to continue believing in God's pleasure intensified. Tiffany was naturally very hard on herself and often linked her critical thoughts about herself to God's thoughts. At one point she started believing that the Lord's grace and mercy didn't apply to her. As a way to fight back against the lies, Tiffany read a daily inspirational quote.

Valentine's Day morning, the quote said something along the lines of, you have a beautiful spirit and soul. Although she expressed little enthusiasm, Tiffany had a sense that God was trying to get her attention. Her response was, "Ok God, that's nice." Tiffany received her love note the night of Valentine's Day and immediately knew it was confirmation from the Lord. She sat and dwelled on His message to her allowing it to sink deep in her heart, affirming what she truly believed.

There were a lot of layers to Tiffany's struggle, as is true for many of us. I didn't know the whole backstory of her childhood; the experiences and parental upbringing that helped shape who she was as a young woman. But God knew, and it was very clear that He wanted her to know and believe the simple truth that He was pleased with her. If we are struggling, the Lord knows it. If we are hurting, He feels it. He alone has the solution to every problem. In fact, He is the solution to every problem. I know that can sound very "churchy" but it's true.

In Tiffany's case, the Lord told her that He was pleased with her more than once, using different means. When He wants a message to get across, He knows how to make it very clear, but He will never force us to believe Him. We have the choice to accept His message/word as the truth or reject it and create a false "truth" on our own terms. Choosing the latter is exactly what the enemy wants us to do. At first, it may seem like the right decision but it will most certainly cause deception, and ultimately end in death.

There is a way that seems right to a man, but its end is the way to death (Proverbs 14:12).

I pray that anyone reading this book who has chosen to create their own "truth" instead of living in obedience to the Holy Word of God will repent and turn to Jesus.

Sjhira Ellzey

Beauty that leaves my heart at rest; never needing to gaze upon another for satisfaction. Those are my thoughts when I look at your sweet face.

*

"I felt like a young girl with her first crush."
-Melissa

*

Melissa was struggling with feelings of insecurity and jealousy towards other women. She compared herself with their looks, how they dressed, and what they had. Other women who had boyfriends were a special sore spot because she had been without one for almost 5 years. Melissa said she would make jokes about it, but deep down inside it was troubling. By January her feelings of animosity were at an all-time high and directed towards her best friend. It was the first time Melissa had ever had negative thoughts about her friend, and in her own words, "The insecurity was like a virus that my immune system could not fight off. That's how I felt."

Melissa read her love note and started crying. It was exactly what she needed to hear. She said, "It's almost like I was hurting Him by not viewing myself the way He saw me." The next morning all feelings of jealousy were gone. She complimented her roommate with a sincere heart. Melissa memorized her love note and recited it back to herself often. She also stored it in her phone and shared it with her mom.

Melissa received her note the evening of February 14th at TSU. That night, after Bible study was over, and I was back home getting ready for bed, I received a text from her that read,

"Just want you to know that you are such a blessing in my life. I love that you have so much faith and that you make no moves in life without God's anointing. I truly do thank you and thank God for you and ask Him to keep you and forever shine in your life. I appreciate you and believe that God purposely placed you in my life, and I thank Him for that. Love you."

Sjhira Ellzey

A bed of rose petals, not enough. A sweet kiss under the Tuscan sun, not good enough. A love song written just for you and sung softly in your ear as you drift asleep...it's just not good enough. You, my love, shall be romanced beyond what the things of this world can offer and I will be the one to romance you.

*

"He's the only one who has the ability to do what He does."
-Mia

*

Mia read her love note and confidently nodded, "He knows me." She was pleased to share that she doesn't view romance the way the world does. She related her note to how an old married couple knows one another. They know what makes the other person happy and they know their unique quirks. Mia said, "Someone is always writing an article or a blog about 101 ways to romance your partner. He knows I don't get excited about that." She then shared an example of how the Lord had romanced her heart. It was through a relationship He brought into her life; her best friend in college. What seemed to be a coincidence of how they met was not a coincidence at all. It was very on purpose, according to Mia, and a powerful expression of God's love towards her.

I love her analogy of an old married couple. Marriage, especially one that has gone through the test of time, develops a depth of love that goes beyond feelings or even intellectual understanding. A husband and wife who stay committed to one another through good times and bad times, in sickness and in health, learn the power of love as sacrifice, repentance, humility, forgiveness, prayer, honor, trust, and perseverance. Sure there are wonderful feelings of ecstasy that are connected to love, but those alone do not establish the foundation.

God is all about relationship and wants to draw our hearts to deeper levels of understanding by the power of the Holy Spirit. When we allow this to happen we stop equating love to that butterfly feeling you get when your crush looks your way and flashes a handsome smile.

Sjhira Ellzey

By definition, via a google search, romance as a noun is a feeling of excitement and mystery associated with love. As a verb it means to woo. An amazing aspect of having a relationship with God is when mysteries are made known to us. The mystery of His love is predictably unpredictable.

We know Jesus died on the cross because of love. We know He is coming back again for His bride. Throughout the Bible we hear Him say I love you over and over and over again. We can predict and have full confidence that Jesus will continue to love us. But the way He goes about doing that is often totally unpredictable. That's why getting to know Him is so exhilarating! He knows us better than we know ourselves. He knows how to love all people perfectly in their own individual way. His love is not generic. You may not know His next move but you know it's going to be good! So, just sit back in his presence, rest, and let the King of kings romance you.

There is joy in my heart I cannot fully explain. It causes my heart to leap, my lips to smile, my soul to sing and my feet to dance. Joy that causes my sorrow to be forgotten and my tears to be no more. This joy goes so deep that nothing will ever be able to take it away. Do you know the source of this joy? Beloved, it is none other than you!

*

"He doesn't love me because He has to, it's because He wants to."
-Sonya

*

At the time Sonya received her love note she was feeling very insecure. Her ex-boyfriend was not happy with her, which led to her thinking, "I can't make anyone happy." Sonya's self-esteem was low and she confessed feeling like she had nothing special or authentic to offer. Once she read her love note, the lie about not being able to make anyone happy was destroyed. She exclaimed, "It's amazing, I make Jesus happy!" Her heart was awakened to God's delight in loving her. It wasn't forced. He wasn't striving. Just pure joy. Sonya kept the love note on her nightstand as a source of constant encouragement.

I would like to point out that her love note contains the word joy, not happiness. There is a difference that I believe is worth noting. An online article by Psychologies (psychologies.co.uk) states, "Joy and happiness are wonderful feelings to experience, but are very different. Joy is more consistent and is cultivated internally. It comes when you make peace with who you are, why you are and how you are, whereas happiness tends to be externally triggered and is based on other people, things, places, thoughts, and events."

There are many scriptures in the Bible that mention joy. I'll mention one of my favorites but I encourage you to dig for more and let the meaning sink in.

We look away from the natural realm and we fasten our gaze onto Jesus who birthed faith within us and who leads us forward into faith's perfection. His example is this: Because his heart was focused on the joy of knowing that you would be his, he endured the agony of the cross and conquered its humiliation, and now sits exalted at the right hand of the throne of God! (Hebrews 12:2 TPT).

I absolutely love this verse. Picture Jesus' bruised and blood drenched body; His hands and feet nailed to the cross; His blood soaked hair matted against His head as blood is streaming down His face. Imagine Him feeling alone and humiliated. Think about Him trying to catch His breath as the organs in His body are shutting down. Honestly, we can only speculate. It is unfathomable to think of what it was really like for Jesus to carry the weight of the world's sin on the cross and then die. And scripture says, *"For the joy set before him he endured the cross..."* What "joy" allowed Him to endure such horrific pain and suffering? You!

Jesus was on a mission. He was laser focused on what had to be done and knew that no one else could do it. As He was in anguish, dying on the cross, He knew that was not the end; it was a new beginning.

The joy of being reunited with His beloved was the Lord's drive and motivation. You are His beloved! Your "yes" to Jesus is His joy! Are you like Sonya, who needed a new perspective on how deeply she moved the heart of God? He leaps, He dances, He smiles, He sings all because of you. Let it sink in and allow His joy to overwhelm your soul. His joy has the ability to carry you through any disappointment, difficult relationship, or other hardship in life. If this joy allowed Him to endure the cross, consider the powerful role you play in His incredible act of sacrificial love.

Just to be close to you is what my heart wants. Just to be close to you is my one desire. Just to be close to you is my true delight. When I am close to you, you take my breath away. I would give my life again...just to be close to you.

*

"How did she know? She just told me to pick a bag!"
-Renee

*

Renee was a believer, but for weeks she had been praying for a closer relationship with God and feeling like nothing was happening. The perceived distance was causing her frustration and stress. Renee's way of dealing with stress was to shut people out because she was an internal processor. She was in her head a lot, not wanting to connect or engage in conversations, often giving one word responses, which caused others to label her as the girl with an attitude who doesn't want to be bothered.

When Renee read her love note she was instantly encouraged and forgot for a split second that I had nothing to do with who received which note. As the realization set in that God was speaking directly to her she exclaimed, "He actually listens to me! He heard me and sent the note through you and gave it to me!" Her confidence was boosted and her frustration/stress was reduced. Renee began reading her Bible more and everyone around her noticed a change in how she interacted with them; no longer having a cold, aloof response.

There seems to be a pattern of thought throughout scripture, in my own life, and in the lives of so many others that I have met; God, where are you? As we are upset and discouraged we fail to realize that the God of all hope has already gone before us to make a way, or that He is actually holding us up with His hand through challenging life moments. *Don't be afraid, for I am with you. Don't be discouraged, for I am your God. I will strengthen you and help you. I will hold you up with my victorious right hand* (Isaiah 41:10 NLT).

When I look back over my life I can see how those difficult moments made me anxious until I saw the manifestation of God's hand working things out.

Then I would suddenly relax and be full of faith again. I would be lying if I said I never get anxious anymore, but the previous challenging times of waiting have exercised my faith and made it stronger. This is a way the Lord helps us to grow in Him. When we are able to go through trials and remain confident in God's Word, even though we don't "feel" or "see" Him, He is greatly pleased.

Dear brothers and sister, when troubles of any kind come your way, consider it an opportunity for great joy. For you know that when your faith is tested your endurance has a chance to grow. So let it grow, for when your endurance is fully developed, you will be perfect and complete, needing nothing (James 1:2-4 NLT). And remember, Satan must flee from a believer who stands firm on the Word of God despite circumstances and human feelings. *Submit yourselves therefore to God. Resist the devil, and he will flee from you* (James 4:7).

Sjhira Ellzey

You are my one true love. You fill my heart in a way that no one else can. There is a deep void without you. I yearn for you. I long for you. I want you and I need you. I want all of you, the good and the bad. Nothing else will do...I want you!

*

"We're supposed to long for Him; to hear Him say He longs for me is just amazing."
-Nicole

*

This endearing message from the Lord went straight to Nicole's heart, filling it with joy. She said it was as if God was sitting right next to her speaking those words. With tears in her eyes, she expressed deep emotion thinking about the Lord forgiving the bad and wanting her just as she was. The longing He had for her almost left her speechless. When she read, "You fill my heart in a way that no one else can," her response was, "That's how I feel about Him." As we were talking, Nicole said she had a specific message, in regard to Valentine's Day, for her peers. "It's ok to be single. Wait on God and be patient. Enjoy this time now, while you are single, because it will be over before you know it."

In terms of personality, Nicole and I were quite the opposite. She was soft-spoken and didn't say much. I was a super out-going, talk to everyone in the room, kind of person. Her quiet strength in the Lord was beautiful to watch and I believe she was a rock for many of her peers. I loved hearing her perspective on the love note. The exchange between her and the Lord was like listening to a couple that gushed love and admiration for one another. It's a wonderful thing to watch how Abba loves on those around you and their response to His love. It makes me fall deeper in love with Him; truly heartwarming!

Sjhira Ellzey

What a beautiful young woman you are; perfect in form and feature. I look at you in awe. How lovely you are to me-every part of you. Let not a man define your beauty but the very words spoken from my heart.

*

"*The timing was perfect!*"
-Felicia

*

Felicia didn't wait for me to set up a time to talk, but called to share her feelings about how specifically God confirmed His word through her love note. Before Valentine's Day, she felt prompted to fast and pray because she had strong feelings for a certain gentleman. Before approaching this man to share her feelings, she heard the Holy Spirit speak to her heart about not letting a man define her worth. When she spoke with the guy he made it clear that the feelings were not mutual. Instead of being devastated, Felicia felt her heart had been protected. The disappointment was there but it wasn't severe. The timing was perfect!

Our hearts are precious to our Heavenly Father. He knows how deep the emotions run and He desires to protect us. How sweet is it that God wanted to reiterate His love and affection for Felicia, even though she had already heard Him, believed Him, and felt comforted by Him. That's just like our Father to continuously pour His love out on us.

Such hope never disappoints us, because God's love has been abundantly poured out within our hearts through the Holy Spirit who was given to us (Romans 5:5 AMP).

Sjhira Ellzey

Beloved, I am near. Though I seem far at times I am closer than you often realize. I will never leave you, never reject you, never abandon you. I will stay close by your side. You can be sure of that.

*

"Wow! How the freak did this happen! I was shocked and felt such joy the entire night. I kept reading the note over and over again!"
-Courtney

*

Out of the corner of my eye I saw someone skipping across the room towards me. It was Courtney! Courtney never skipped but this particular night she skipped up to me with sheer delight all over her face and said, "Sjhira, Sjhira, look which one I got!"

I was shocked as I watched her jump up and down like a little child. Simultaneously, goose bumps covered my arms and pure joy flooded my soul as I read the words, *"Beloved, I am near."* An hour before Bible study that same night, Courtney expressed concern about feeling like God was very distant. This bothered her for some time and was preventing her spiritual growth. She had become so discouraged with the lack of feeling God's presence while reading her Bible, or during worship.

Many times in a corporate worship setting when people made reference to feeling the awesome presence of God, Courtney couldn't feel anything. She began to fear that God had left her and was feeling defeated, as so many of us have felt before. From a spiritual perspective, she was sluggishly walking with her head down low, losing hope fast. But then the God of all hope reached down and gently lifted her head, touched her heart, and infused her soul with His truth, *"Just as I was with Moses, so I will be with you. I will not leave you or forsake you,"* (Joshua 1:5).

Receiving this timely word from the Lord changed everything. Courtney's heart drew closer to God as she began to see Him differently. Revelations were continually filling her heart. She was instantly comforted, knowing that Jesus is with her at all times even when she doesn't feel His presence.

"He has put truth in me. I know He is always there and now I am more at peace!"

There was a time when I was experiencing several days of significant anxiety. When I prayed for peace, I still felt anxious. Since I'm not one to struggle with panic attacks or constant anxiety I decided to pray and fast. My prayer was for the Lord to not only surround me with His peace, but to instruct me on how to move forward. On the third day of my fast the Holy Spirit simply told me to focus on what's inside and not my surroundings. I immediately knew what He meant as His perfect peace clothed me. The Spirit of the Lord is living in each of us who are called by His name. There will be times when we don't "feel" God. There will be times when He seems distant. It is in those times that we must remember His unchanging Word keeps us anchored. Then we can confidently declare, as Courtney did, that He has put truth in me! The Holy Spirit also said to me, *"Sjhira, don't just read my Word; eat it. Drink it."* May we continue to feast on living food and water for the nourishment of our souls!

You are my hidden treasure and I have the key that unlocks your precious jewels. No key shall be given to the unworthy. I have the key and I alone will choose who is worthy to partake of my precious treasure, that is you.

*

"I am a secret nobody has discovered."
-Willow

*

Willow read her love note and knew it was from God. The way He described her as a treasure made her feel very special because treasures are highly valuable and sought after. The "jewels" were her emotions, thoughts, heart; every part that made up who she was. As we talked, Willow shared how she has the propensity to hand over her jewels to those who don't deserve them or mistreat them. In other words, the "unworthy." Her strong sensitivity and empathy often overwhelm her, and as a result, she is quick to share herself with others without considering who is being letting in.

Sjhira Ellzey

After reading the note she understood that God wanted to protect her. Like most of the young women who received a love note, Willow was trying to navigate through the dating scene and wondered who she would end up marrying. Many Christian women in college question the Lord on who is "the one." For Willow, this love note confirmed that God wanted her to release control and trust Him for her future spouse. He also wanted her to trust Him on all levels of relationship with others, not just the romantic ones. She was deeply comforted that the Lord knew who would be "worthy."

When we think of a treasure most of us would picture gold coins, diamonds, precious stones, fine jewelry, etc... that has been hidden someplace for someone specific. Many movies depict the thrill of a treasure hunt. Someone finds a map, usually the good guy, with directions on how to find a great buried treasure. But then to add some drama a villain shows up on the scene to try and get to the treasure first, and will certainly kill anyone in his/her way. Movies do a great job of presenting an exhilarating, mostly feel-good story that allows us to check-out of reality for about 2 hours. The truth is, this concept of a "treasure hunt" is very much our reality as we see it woven throughout the Bible.

You are a treasure. Satan is the villain trying to steal from you, destroy you, and kill you. God made a way, through Jesus, for you to be safe and hidden in Him. The whole purpose of life on earth is to love God, understanding that we are His beloved creation - His treasure, and to love others as we love ourselves. Accept His free gift of reconciliation, through the blood of Jesus, and love people so they too will know Him and understand their invaluable worth in His eyes.

Sjhira Ellzey

Sweetness, you are sweet to the touch, to the eye, and none compares to you. Sweeter than a summer's breeze, sweeter than a fragrance that makes a man weak in his knees. Sweeter than a field of wild-flowers or a bushel of roses. Sweetness that lingers and is enjoyed by all, but most importantly it is enjoyed by me.

*

"Wow, I'm touched. God really thinks I'm sweet!"
-Norah

*

Leading up to Valentine's Day, Norah had been struggling with feelings of inferiority, especially the day before. These feelings were mostly connected to her appearance, personality, and relationships. One of her biggest fears was that her boyfriend would find someone better. And so, there was Norah on Valentine's Day with a boyfriend whom she couldn't enjoy because of the fear of rejection.

Then she received a note with a sweet message from God, who was very aware of the condition of her heart. His beloved didn't know her worth. Norah needed to be reminded she was special and that there were unique aspects to her personality that stood out.

When she read, "None compares to you," she instantly felt the deep encouragement from the One who actually created her. The word "sweet" breathed life directly into her personality as she had been known to carry a "sweetness." This love note to Norah was reassuring her that people liked being around her, which could have very well included her boyfriend. But it is clear that the Lord is saying His delight in her "sweetness" surpasses anyone else's opinion, therefore, even if she feels inferior to another person or rejected by her boyfriend, God's perspective is most important.

The struggle with low self-image and low self-esteem is common among college women across this nation and all over the world. During this time many dating relationships form because of the exploratory age and the nature of the environment. This can be done in a healthy way if you are spiritually mature and ready to consider the nuances of two people joining as one in a marriage union. But let's face it, our individualistic, independent, and sexually promiscuous culture doesn't support that kind of maturity. Most 18-22 year olds are simply not ready for a healthy dating relationship. It is also very tempting to compare yourselves to others, which can be exhausting. You will always be able to find someone who is smarter, has something you want, receives more attention, or in your eyes looks better than you. We all need the reminder that Norah received from God; we are unique, we are special, and He is most delighted in us.

The perfect sunset, the early sunrise, the radiant sparkle of a rainbow, the intensity of the blue Caribbean Sea, the most delicate petal, the fragrance after the rain, the twinkle of a starry sky on a clear night, the brilliance of a perfectly cut diamond...my love, none of that even compares to you.

*

"It was a different Valentine's Day for me."
-Elise

*

Elise admitted that she hated Valentine's Day. From her perspective, it was not a day to celebrate unless you had a man. When she arrived at Bible study the night of February 13th, she had already decided to have a bad attitude the following day. Little did she know, the Lord had other plans!

Elise read her note and her strong negativity dissolved. She felt so special as her spirit filled with peace. As Elise re-read her note, the Holy Spirit imparted to her a powerful revelation about material things not being a true source of joy, whether it came in the form of a new out-fit or a boyfriend. As the revelation was sinking in, Elise said, "All I need is God. He wants me to fall in love with Him with my whole heart, not just half of it."

From that moment, Elise knew she was going to have a different Valentine's Day! Moving forward, she continued to perceive life differently, no longer placing a strong emphasis on material things, but resting more in God's perfect love.

I have to say, Elise's negativity about Valentine's Day surprised me. She was a girly-girl type; makeup done, hair always styled, and wore cute outfits. Admittedly, I thought she would be one of those ladies who lays out the perfect red or pink outfit the night before while making Valentine's Day cookies for everyone on her hall. I was way off!

Her initial negative comments along with some of the other students' is what prompted me to go before the Lord with a heavy heart and ask for help. Had I not done that, I probably would have been the one making cookies to pass out at Bible Study. Thankfully, Elise was honest. She didn't just brush it off like it was no big deal. It wasn't just another day for her. It was a reminder that she didn't have a man and that made her mad! The Lord could hear the cry of Elise's heart and He responded to her. A simple utterance from His heart to hers is all it took for her to have a new outlook and enjoy the sweetness of a new day.

Sjhira Ellzey

My dear, when I made you I was speechless. Such an exquisite creation; delicately molded by my very hands. All of Heaven watched as I made you. It was a site to behold and to this day you leave me breathless at the very thought of you.

*

"That builds something in my heart that I cannot even explain."
-Victoria

*

For a woman who has never met her father, to hear God doting over her like a proud dad is very difficult to believe. In a nutshell, that was Victoria's initial response. The pain of not knowing her father was there but it was suppressed, and she admitted she lived life "in denial" to the depth of that pain. Instead of dwelling on a natural "fatherlessness," her more prominent thoughts were about Jesus not being in her past or paying special attention to her, and she wondered if God was proud of her.

In hindsight, Victoria was able to look back over her life and confess that she had carried a broken heart and struggled with self-worth and rejection. But that confession didn't come until truth was uncovered. Little did Victoria know that this love note was going to trigger a ripple effect of healing in her soul.

Soon after reading the note, one of her pastors spoke a message on broken hearts. As painful feelings connected to her father began to surface, Victoria started sobbing. Her heart was broken. She felt unforgiveness, wanting to forgive her father for abandonment but couldn't in her own strength.

Victoria asked God for a new heart that would be able to forgive. Then she was reminded of a prophetic word she received at 14yrs old: *"Nothing is in vain. When I made you I put my stamp on you when you were born. I offered you as a sweet smelling sacrifice to God. All of Heaven acknowledged that you were born for purpose."* As Victoria surrendered her heart to the Lord, He breathed life, affirmation, and confidence. The Lord was confirming His presence not only at her birth, but throughout her life. She sensed that God cared for her. Describing her in the love note with the word "exquisite" was a way to build up her confidence that she was unique and had something special to offer.

Victoria and I spoke about her love note several days after the pastor's message and all the revelation and healing that took place. Earlier that morning, she looked through her baby pictures and with a happy heart pictured God there, present in her early life. The deep feelings of rejection and abandonment were being replaced with a belief that her life was wanted, by God, and she was here on purpose.

Victoria said to me, "I think God is trying to fill up my cup." As I was listening to her story, it was like watching a puzzle coming together piece by piece. I simply shared my thoughts that she had been relating to God the Father, as if He was her natural father, because that's all she knew to do. But God was not her natural father and wanted to renew her understanding of "daddy." With tears in her eyes, Victoria's response to me was, "I take that as a word of knowledge and encouragement. That builds something in my heart that I cannot even explain."

The theme of fatherlessness is recurring throughout this book. After hearing the stories connected to the love notes it was very clear that many young ladies were struggling with fatherlessness. This is very important to God because we will relate to Him as we relate to our natural father. Our natural father is meant to be a direct example of The Father's love. Those without a healthy example will need divine revelation and deep healing in order to see God as a loving father and relate to Him in such a way. My heart was deeply encouraged to see how the Lord continued to address this issue. God was drawing hearts to Him to heal and restore. New identities were being rebuilt!

If you struggle relating to God as a loving Father, read the following as a direct message from His heart to yours and put your name on the line.

_____, I knew you before I even formed you and my eyes were fixed on you the day that you were born. I smiled as my heart experienced great delight in gazing upon something so beautiful. Look what I created! My dear, I have taken a front row seat in your life. Your first giggle made me giggle. I cheered when you took your first step. I was there when you fell and scraped your knee. I have been there from the beginning and I'm right here, right now. Daddy is here!

Heart Expressions from the Throne Room

I want to be your knight in shining armor. I want to rescue you from a tower like when a maiden waits for her prince and he comes to take her away from all that is dangerous. Come with me and be my maiden, the one whom my heart adores. I have fought for you because your love was worth the fight. Just to have you in my arms again was worth the fight.

*

"Even creation doesn't confound me as much as God's love. How high, deep, long, and wide...it's beyond me."
-Cynthia

*

Cynthia faithfully attended our weekly campus Bible study. She was the cutest little thing; small in stature and showed very little emotion; almost boredom. If we didn't know any better, we would have thought we were wasting her time. I chuckle as I write this because I'm picturing Cynthia's face before she received the love note and then after. She admitted to me that she didn't think she needed people. She had an "I can handle that," or "I got this," mentality. We could have easily given her the nickname, Miss Independent.

Sjhira Ellzey

This particular love note going to Cynthia proves that God has a sense of humor and can use any method of His choosing to get one's attention. For example, little girls often dress up and pretend to be princesses, but as a little girl Cynthia would have considered that foolish; not giving any thought to a "knight in shining armor," or "my prince." If you gave 5 year-old Cynthia the option of watching Sleeping Beauty or working on a Rubik's cube, she would have chosen the latter.

When we spoke about her love note she was dumbfounded, and to be honest it was quite amusing. There were times when it seemed like she was blushing as she spoke about the intensity of God's love for her. In those brief moments, I saw more emotion come out of that girl than I had seen in the past year!

Cynthia started off by saying, "Sjhira, few things confound me. The love of God confounds me." And with that, she began dissecting each part and sharing how it was the perfect message to awaken her heart. Cynthia mentioned how every girl has a part in her that wants her prince, and through the love note,

God revealed to her that area of her heart. "He wants me more than I can imagine. He wants me to know I can't do it on my own and it's ok to need Him. I'm realizing that I actually need Him."

The Holy Spirit showed Cynthia how a knight has a shield, armor, and a sword...everything for her protection. No one and nothing can stand against the glory of God. She said, "He is my strong tower; my confidence knowing He is near." When the Lord said, *"Come with me,"* she pictured them running away together as she left her worries and cares behind. The smile on Cynthia's face when she mentioned how He fought for her was a beautiful glimpse of the condition of her heart. The Lord was wooing her. He was winning her over.

If I had taken matters in my own hands and handed the love notes out, knowing who was going to get which note, I would have never in a million years given this note to Cynthia. In fact, I may have given in to the intimidation of her "bored" look and made an excuse as to why she didn't have to take a love note if she didn't want to. Thankfully, I serve a God who is much bigger than me and He knows best! He had a plan all along. He knows our hearts and He alone knows how to pursue us. Cynthia's story reminds me of a song:

> You've won my affection
> You've captured my heart
> You have my devotion
> My worship is yours
>
> You've won my affection
> You've captured my heart
> Now I am yours
> Completely yours, forever

My heart is awakened by your beauty at the rising sun. A smile forms on my lips as I see you awake from your slumber. There is no flaw in what my eyes see and my heart is falling deeper in love with you at each passing day.

*

"*Oh my God! Wow, this is for me? Wow, this is so beautiful! So poetic and romantic.*"
-Yolanda

*

Yolanda was not only a student but a mama to a 3-year old boy. At the time she received her love note she was going through, what she called, "a self-image re-evaluation." She had just been on the phone with a guy friend and literally asked him what was wrong with her body. Even after 3 years Yolanda was still trying to adjust to her post-baby body and she had recently gotten a new haircut. She was being very hard on herself; scrutinizing every little detail about her image, including her smile.

The love note came at the perfect time. Yolanda was overwhelmed by how specific the Lord was speaking to her. She said, "At that moment I needed to hear that I was beautiful."

Yolanda's self-image was strengthened. God's word breathed truth to a question she had in her heart, and as a result she was refreshed. I love how this message from the Lord is about Yolanda as she is first waking up. I'm pretty sure we can all agree that we don't look our best when we first wake up. We have eye crusties, bed-head, pillow lines on our face, and possibly drool running down the side of our mouths, if it was good sleep. Yet, the Lord spoke to Yolanda about her incredible beauty as she wakes! Could it be that God sees something that you don't see? Could it be that God's standard of beauty is very different from the world's standard? And could it be that He wants to teach you how to see through His eyes?

Every single moment you are thinking of me! How precious and wonderful to consider that you cherish me constantly in your every thought! O God, your desires toward me are more than the grains of sand on every shore! When I awake each morning, you're still with me (Psalm 139:17-18 TPT).

Ah yes, the day you were born I danced. I danced...there was such joy in my heart I did not know what else to do. Will you dance with me my darling? It does not matter who is looking. I just want to dance with you and celebrate your glorious life!

*

"*I know He loves me, but God actually likes me!*"
-Hailee

*

Almost in disbelief, Hailee found it hard to fathom that she could make the Lord so happy that He wanted to dance! "What makes Him that excited?"

Hailee was a quiet and shy young lady. The sweetness of the Lord asking her to dance brought a smile to her face. Hailee said, "I see Him asking me to dance like a gentleman." After a pause she said she would dance with Him, but would be reluctant with her head down. Hailee also connected "dancing" to her life purpose but questioned what that would look like. "How do you want me to dance with you? How does my life show a dance?" Those were great questions that I hope Hailee sought the answers to!

Sjhira Ellzey

My goodness, I love the image of the Lord, a gentleman, standing in front of Hailee, a shy woman with her head down, offering His hand to her with the invitation to dance. God is not forceful with us. He is polite. He invites us to Him and waits patiently. The image continues as I picture the Lord's outstretched hand gently lifting Hailee's chin so that their eyes meet. She is now fixed on His gaze and the shyness dissipates as the love He has for her overwhelms her entire being. Hailee confidently accepts the invitation to dance with her Lord, the lover of her soul, and they float across the dance floor without a care in the world. Her eyes never leave His. She is totally content, full of joy and completely free!

The Lord said to Hailee, *"It doesn't matter who is looking."* God is continually teaching us to stop focusing on others in an unhealthy way. We need to stop the comparisons. We should not be focused on what others are thinking about us and/or trying to live a man-pleasing life. If the Lord is pleased, that is enough. He alone is more than enough. His thoughts about us outnumber the grains of sand! What would have happened if Hailee declined the Lord's invitation due to the embarrassment of who was looking? If we look at it from the perspective of this dance being connected to her purpose or calling, what would have happened if she said no?

    The Lord has a way of bringing us out of our comfort zone in order to experience Him. When He calls us to live for Him, it will require trust. He leads the dance in life and we follow His steps. When dancing with a partner, one person is the leader. When the partner lets go and allows the leader to lead the dance is smooth, beautiful, and loads of fun! We must come to the end of ourselves so that God's purpose in our lives reaches its highest potential. Do you see His hand stretched out to you? What will be your response when He asks *you* to dance?

Sjhira Ellzey

Oh won't you please allow me to hold your face gently in the palm of my hands and softly kiss you? A kiss of purity and wholeness that will leave your heart deeply satisfied; never again restless or disturbed. A kiss that brings freedom, not bondage. A kiss you will want to remember and never forget.

*

"*I never thought God would express love like this...*"
-*Morgan*

*

When Morgan and I first began talking I could sense her discomfort. After reading her love note she was confused, felt uneasy, and was reluctant to talk about it. Honestly, I don't remember what I said because this was over 10 years ago, but knowing myself, I probably re-read the note out loud and asked how she was feeling.

Within a matter of moments, I witnessed a very delicate process of unwinding. At first Morgan was similar to that of a tightly wound spool of thread, however, as we talked through the different parts of her love note, the thread began to loosen. Our time together blew me away as I watched the Holy Spirit unravel her soul by bringing back memories and gently revealing truth.

The ball got rolling when Morgan first admitted that the topic of kissing brought up negative emotions from her past, and how weird it was to think of God expressing His love like this. Understandably, she attached kissing to humans. Morgan had been in a 2-year relationship that was over. When she and the ex-boyfriend kissed, she confessed it felt so wrong and impure that she told him she didn't want to kiss anymore. Consequently, the terms "restless" and "disturbed" were accurate words to describe how she felt about those kisses.

During that timeframe she often daydreamed about kisses she would enjoy, and the image she saw was of her husband holding her face and kissing her forehead or cheek. As Morgan spoke, I had to contain my excitement! The connection between her love note and what she was sharing was almost more than I could bear, but I waited as the wheels turned in her mind. This was her time and the Lord was obviously at work.

The way God was showing His love to Morgan was different from what she had ever experienced in relationship with Him, and it was taking time to process. By the end of our conversation, there was a little smile forming as she took a deep breath and began unpacking this revelation; kisses from the Lord are pure. They are good and will not make me feel impure.

When I heard the Lord speak this love note I remember thinking, "Whoa! He's using something as human and intimate as kissing to express His heart!" I also remember the image He gave me of holding a woman's face in the palm of His hands and kissing her forehead. I did not see Morgan's face, until I found out that this was her love note.

After learning that this was an area of her soul that needed healing, my heart swelled at the fact that Jesus lovingly asked for her permission to kiss her. The freedom she needed was right in front of her with a warm invitation. God was present when Morgan and her boyfriend were kissing. Everything we do, think, and say is recorded (if that doesn't produce a Holy fear of the Lord, I don't know what will).

God doesn't miss one moment of our lives. He sees everything and is embarrassed by nothing. He could see with laser focus how unsettled Morgan was by those kisses. And even when she suppressed the negative feelings and "forgot," God didn't forget. He knew there was a better way for her. Jesus wanted Morgan to be able to enjoy something pure and beautiful that He created, kissing! Deliverance was needed and He already had it planned out.

The Lord is such a gentleman. He doesn't force His way into our lives. He simply makes Himself available and His intentions known. The Lord kneels before us with His arms open wide and invites us to run to Him. This image reminds me of Jesus' time on earth. He came here because He knew we were lost, broken, confused, sick, and in desperate need of a savior. But the way He came was different from what people were expecting. The awaited Savior was born into the world as a baby? Not rich? Not attractive?

Breaking the rules? Surely God, the King of kings, would not express His love and great power in this way!

Many people looked Jesus directly in the eyes, literally saw His arms open and walked away because they couldn't believe the Savior of the world would reveal Himself in this odd way. Others looked Him in the eyes, saw His open arms and jumped right in. What will be your response?

I anticipate that the Lord has tons of kisses that He is just longing to plant all over our faces. When my son, who is a toddler with fat cheeks and big pouty lips, gets sick of me kissing his face and says, "Mama, no more kisses please," I can back off for a moment, but then I get this irresistible urge to start kissing him again! I cannot fathom what it would feel like if my son considered my kisses to be disturbing or made him feel restless. In this way I can kind of relate to the heart of the Father who desires us to be whole. He has so much of Himself to give.

There is much to be enjoyed by knowing God but we can't receive all that He has for us if we remain broken. We have to give Him access to those broken, sick, and dead areas in our lives so that He can restore us to our original design. On earth, that will be a continual process because we live in a fallen world and our bodies are a temporary form of housing. But in Glory, it will be permanent! And just to be clear, the kisses from God can start now! Please don't make Him wait until you leave this earth to let Him start kissing you!

Sjhira Ellzey

Your tears are beautiful to me. I have each one saved in a jar. I will never forget those times you cried. My precious one, I was there collecting your tears. I care when no one else cares. I'm present when everyone is gone. I listen when no one else listens. Tears are not forgotten, they are collected, and you are restored.

*

"So many things are running through my head. I've lost so much sleep."
-Amanda

*

College was supposed to be the great escape for Amanda; an escape from a very stressful and depressing home life that caused many nights of crying herself to sleep. Younger siblings struggled with major behavioral problems, putting a lot of stress on her mom. Her father did not live in the home with them and he thought Amanda only needed him for his money. Consequently, all of her mother's attention was on the difficulties of coping with single-parenthood. There was no time for Amanda, and watching her mother so stressed out caused her grief.

She was giving so much of herself and not receiving anything in return that it made her exhausted. With a heaviness in her voice, Amanda said, "I'm tired of people expecting so much from me."

Unfortunately, college was not the escape Amanda hoped it would be. At first, everything seemed fine. She started off going to church, something she had done regularly as a little girl. One Sunday she woke up too tired to go, and then every Sunday after she was too tired. Amanda admitted it was so easy to serve and worship God as a little girl but as an adult it was tiring and overwhelming.

Then she experienced a breakup with her boyfriend that she admitted was very hard to get over. Before receiving her love note, the most recent struggle she had faced was a fall-out with her close friend. The fall-out happened during the 2006 holiday season, so by Valentine's Day 2007, Amanda's heart was heavy and burdened. In response to those difficulties she confessed, "No one understands or knows what I'm dealing with."

Amanda was comforted that her tears were seen, acknowledged and collected. She was obviously experiencing difficult life situations that don't correct themselves with the snap of a finger, or even after receiving a love note from Jesus. Her siblings were still behaving poorly and stressing her mother out. Her relationship with her boyfriend was still over. Her relationship with the close friend was still rocky, and her dad still thought he was just a bank. But God knew all of that.

The Lord's message to Amanda was not, I'm going to zap everyone and everything around you so all your problems go away. He spoke to her heart simply saying, *"I'm here, I understand and I care...your grief has not gone unnoticed."* And then He leaves her with a promise that she will be restored. How? When? We don't know. But it can and will happen. He's the God of hope.

Now may God, the inspiration and fountain of hope, fill you to overflowing with uncontainable joy and perfect peace as you trust in him. And may the power of the Holy Spirit continually surround your life with his super-abundance until you radiate with hope! (Romans 15:13 TPT).

It's precious to me that the Lord didn't go into the how's and when's with her. It's as if He just sat down beside her, put His hand on her back and said, *"Honey, I'm here and I know you're hurting."* Sometimes that's all we need in order to step into faith to believe for brighter days ahead. If/when you find yourself in a similar place that Amanda was in, my hope is that you will know you have a God who is present, who cares for you, and who has the ability to carry you through every trial of life. He is collecting your tears and one day He will wipe them all away.

Listen to me, descendants of Jacob, all who remain in Israel. I have cared for you since you were born. Yes, I carried you before you were born. I will be your God throughout your lifetime - until your hair is white with age. I made you, and I will care for you. I will carry you along and save you. (Isaiah 46:3-4 NLT).

Sjhira Ellzey

Do you know how special you are to me? If I took a lifetime to explain that to you, time would run out and I would have just begun. That is why I have eternity with you on my heart. For an eternity I will show you how special you are to me...and I will never be able to stop.

*

"He will fully be able to show me how special and unique I am."
-Karyn

*

Karyn grew up going to church and accepted Jesus as Lord and Savior at a young age. She was told many times throughout her childhood about the anointing of God on her life, however, there was a hidden place in her heart that lacked confidence in her story. She believed that a powerful testimony entailed someone who had experienced trauma, great danger, perversion, abuse, addiction, etc..., and then met Jesus and got delivered. And all the "good" church boys and girls, like herself, had nothing special to share. In fact, she used the word "boring" to describe her testimony.

After reading her love note she felt like God was speaking directly to that hidden place in her heart. "Puts me back on track and gives me hope and assurance that He will fully be able to show me how special and unique I am. I am special. That is what keeps me fighting this fight."

Growing up in the church is a wonderful thing, but let's be honest, it can also produce some pretty funky misconceptions about God and His Word. For instance, many early church goers, like Karyn, learn to rank sins because, from the pulpit, some seem to get a slap on the hand while others are completely condemned. Not sharing with your siblings is not nice. Lying to your parents is bad. Cheating on your test at school is wrong but somehow justifiably ok if you're not caught (sarcastic tone). Stealing from a store is really bad and shameful. Murder and adultery...that's it, you're going to hell, sinner!

Throughout scripture it is clear that sin is sin and God hates it. Sure, there are different consequences to sin, and from a worldly standpoint some consequences are worse and more shameful than others. But the bottom line is as stated in the book of Romans,

"What then? Are we Jews any better off? No, not at all! For we have already charged that all, both Jews and Greeks, are under sin...all have turned aside; together they have become worthless; no one does good, not even one...for all have sinned and fall short of the glory of God..." (Romans 3:9,12,23).

For the wages of sin is death (Romans 6:23).

In a very sick and twisted religious way, our flesh likes to focus on everyone else around us that we can frown upon to somehow make ourselves feel better. I may be doing this but at least I'm not doing *that,* or in another sick and twisted religious way, we may just shrug our shoulders in boredom. Holding on to either one of those mindsets is a trick of the enemy because it will keep you from discerning the movement of Heaven in your life.

We must first recognize and admit that we are all sinners and we all deserve spiritual death. When we understand the true depravity of our souls without Jesus and His gift of eternal life, the power of His love envelops our entire being. The focus is lifted off of ourselves and placed entirely on Jesus, so, no matter the circumstances, we know that we are special and have a powerful story in Christ! It is then, and only then, that we are able to connect with the heartbeat of God; receiving His love and then loving others.

Sjhira Ellzey

I know your heart. I know your desire to be the most beautiful bride man has laid his eyes on. Well, my dear, I see your wedding day and I, your husband, think you are most beautiful indeed!

*

"It fits me so well because God knows my desires."
-Mikaela

*

Mikaela admitted that she was "pissed off" on Valentine's Day; having an attitude all day long. When she received her love note her mood lightened. Mikaela was moved by the truth that the Lord knows every detail about her. He not only knows her needs but He is also aware of her desires. She said, "He knows things I don't even recognize about myself."

Reading this love note after spending the day in such a bad mood caused Mikaela's thoughts to shift off herself; off her current frustrations and onto a very powerful and loving God. He captured her attention and put her mind at ease as she thought about how His thoughts for her are above anyone else's thoughts.

We all have desires that go unshared but God knows them. In fact, He knows what we will want and think about before we do. Many of our desires come from Him in the first place and He knows how to present them to us in the right way and in His perfect timing. It is also possible to have a strong desire that the Lord puts in our heart that we imagine being given to us in a way that He never intended. This may cause confusion, not because God is trying to confuse us but because we want it our way instead of trusting His way.

During this time in my life, working as a campus missionary, the Lord told me 3 times to ask Him for a very specific desire of my heart. He wanted me to call the desire out by name and ask Him for it. I was resisting at first because I didn't want to admit how deep the desire went, which is why He had to tell me 3 times. I finally let my guard down and gushed my heart out before the Father in detail. I didn't hold anything back and felt a powerful release once I was truly honest. I was also anticipating how the Lord was going to bring about the manifestation of this specific desire. After all, He wanted me to ask Him for it so of course that meant He was going to give it to me, right?

In this case, about a month after I laid my heart out bare before the Lord, His answer to me was no. If you're like me your jaw just dropped. Why in the world would God feel so strongly in wanting me to ask Him for something that He wasn't going to give me. That sounds mean.

For months I questioned Him on this and did not receive an answer. I felt confused and hurt but continued seeking Him because I believed He was good; from His Word and from past experience. About 7 months later, I woke up early in the morning to pray and journal and I heard the Holy Spirit say, *do you want to know why I told you to ask me for that desire?* Umm, YES PLEASE!!!!

Just like a father talking to his daughter, the Lord began telling me how much He loves to hear the sound of my voice. He told me how He sees and knows the depths of my thoughts and feelings. He also said that He wants the kind of relationship with me where I feel the absolute freedom to approach Him and share those thoughts and feelings. Like a little girl who sits on her daddy's lap, looks him in the eyes and says with a great big smile, daddy, I want a pony! Or a 17-year-old girl who throws herself in her dad's arms, buries her head in his chest and cries because her boyfriend thinks it's best if they are just friends. His heart is tender towards His beloved.

The Holy Spirit said to me, *"Sjhira, when you come to me and pour your heart out, my heart is moved. I want you to know you may come to me and ask me for anything. You are my daughter and I am your Father. I also know what is best for you and have a marvelous plan unfolding right before your eyes! Your heart is precious to me. You don't have to hide it or act like those things weighing on your heart are unimportant. I know and I care. I am a good Father and I give good gifts to my children. If you ask me for something and I do not give it to you it's because I know what is best and my best for you has already been set in motion before the foundation of the world. Continue to remain vulnerable before me and I will protect you. I want you to trust me, even when you don't understand. Trust my love for you."*

Ever since then, I was awakened to a new area of God's heart. All the prior hurt, confusion, and disappointment rolled off me like water on the back of a duck. What I didn't share is that the same desire the Lord said no to was actually given to me. You see, the Lord specifically said no to how I wanted the desire to present itself but the root of the desire was fulfilled in His perfect way and along with it has come eternal satisfaction!

I know many of you reading this book are carrying similar disappointments. Let my story be an encouragement to you that God's heart is pure and full of love. He knows what He is doing. Just wait on Him and in the meantime enjoy the relationship.

There is no phrase in the human language eloquent enough to express my love for you. For this reason, I love you from my heart in a way that is unexplainable and leaves you speechless and in awe. In silence you will hear the whispers of my love language, specifically constructed for the secret places of your heart to understand.

*

"For something to leave me speechless and in awe must be very profound."
-Charlotte

*

Talk about speaking someone's language! Charlotte was an English major who loved reading, words, and effective communication. She also enjoyed analytical thinking and talking things through as a form of processing. I remember having discussions with Charlotte about God, life, etc... . She had an extensive vocabulary and loved asking questions. The best way I can describe our conversations is that they were very collegiate. I'm sure her professors loved having her in class!

When Charlotte read her note her eyebrows raised and she responded, "Wow God, you love me that much!" She was amazed by how directly the Lord spoke to her.

Voicing her thoughts on most matters came easy to Charlotte, but there was one topic she avoided: love. Interestingly enough, the Lord's love note sparked that conversation. A month after Valentine's Day Charlotte attended a Christian conference for college students. On the 5+ hour bus ride she said there were moments of stillness when she could feel God's love and peace comforting and reassuring her.

For Charlotte this was significant because she had been feeling sad about a previous breakup with her boyfriend several months before. She admitted, "I think about love a lot but I don't talk about it." Charlotte grew up going to a church that did not focus on the topic of love. Consequently, in a Christian setting like college campus Bible study, that was not an area of conversation she felt free to engage in. She would often think about getting married and finding the right spouse without having to compromise her morals and specific preferences. She found herself asking, "God, is this possible?" Charlotte told me that one of the songs we sang at the conference made a huge impression on her heart. These are the lyrics that moved her:

> Love is more than a word
> Love is more than a song
> Love is more than riches and gold
> Love is a man who died for his own

As she allowed revelation to set in, Charlotte said, "I already have love because God is love." She felt special because God was listening to her prayers and knew the inner most desires of her heart. With a new sense of hope she said, "He really does care about those things."

Remember how I told you the Lord spoke only one person's name to me after the love note was written? Well, this was it! I knew this note was for Charlotte but the Lord told me not to hand it to her and to trust Him. My direction was to conceal every love note in a brown paper bag and hand them out blindly, which is what I did.

Fast forward to February 13th, a Tuesday night at Fisk. There were 18 ladies at Bible Study that night so I randomly picked 18 brown paper bags out of my trunk and put them on a table. The students eagerly picked a bag and my heart was racing as I watched Charlotte open hers. Can you imagine my anticipation as I walked over to find out which love note she had received? She showed me and I yelled out, while jumping up and down, "Charlotte got the note! Oh my gosh, she got it!"

The energy in that room was electric as the Holy Spirit downloaded His presence and truth in our hearts. I thought I was just going to be a spectator in this mighty move of God, but His plans were greater! That moment for me was like receiving my own love note with the message, *"Sjhira, my love, I know how much you love surprises and I know how to give the best ones. Continue to trust me throughout your life and watch how I will blow you away. I told you I could*

Heart Expressions from the Throne Room

get the love note to Charlotte (wink)! Thank you for your obedience!"

Sjhira Ellzey

Elegance...the way you carry yourself, the way you walk and talk is elegant. You are a true woman in the perfect way I made you. You grace the world with your elegance, but most importantly you grace the heart of your King.

*

"Wow, the wording is amazing! I'm kind of speechless."
-Crystal

*

This was not the first time Crystal had been told she was elegant. She actually heard it her entire life. This time, however, was different. Hearing that she was elegant from God himself and the way it was worded made her speechless. Her eyes got really big when she read out loud, *"You are a true woman in the perfect way I made you."* Crystal felt honored, joyful, and full of peace as she reflected on the Lord's message to her. She also gave Him the credit by saying, "He made me this way. I'm living out the design He has placed in me." Crystal was prompted to pray that God would be reflected through her as a light from her heart and soul so that others would see Him and be encouraged.

The Holy Spirit used this love note to confirm a very powerful message Crystal had been hearing her entire life. People were seeing a beautiful characteristic of God so strongly through her and it was clearly meant to be shared, not for Crystal's gain but for the Glory of the Lord! We all carry unique characteristics of God that are meant to be seen and shared. We are His creation; bearers of His image! Isn't that incredible? When we surrender our hearts to Jesus and are reconciled back to our Creator, the foggy mirror clears and we begin to see ourselves the way He sees us. We also begin to see others through His eyes and can appreciate His beauty in new ways.

As a daughter of the King, what characteristics of your Father do others notice through you? Are you confident in these divine qualities you possess? What about your identity as a woman? How do you feel about that? As far as I know Crystal didn't struggle with her identity as a young lady, but I find it fascinating that the phrase, *"You are a true woman in the perfect way I made you,"* got her attention as she responded, "That's a strong statement!" God made no mistakes when He created man and then woman.

So God created man in his own image, in the image of God he created him; male and female he created them (Genesis 1:27).

He knew what He was doing and He did it perfectly. Many people today are struggling with confusion as it pertains to their gender and identity. That confusion does not come from the Lord. If any part of your heart has difficulty accepting your God-given design as a woman and you want help, take a moment before continuing this book and go to your Creator. Be honest with Him. Talk to Him like He's sitting right there with you on the couch. Tell Him your thoughts. Tell Him about the struggle. Then ask Jesus to speak directly to you and be prepared to listen. Pray for supernatural revelation and divine understanding. Jesus will only speak truth because He is truth.

I am the way, and the truth, and the life. No one comes to the Father except through me (John 14:6).

And you will know the truth, and the truth will set you free (John 8:32).

If something extraordinary doesn't happen at the moment you pray, don't be discouraged. We tend to look for a lightning bolt response from God in order to believe that He's moving in our midst. If He wants to zap you right now, He can and He will, but He may take you through a process or lead you on a beautiful journey of healing. Either way, continue to keep your heart open and honest before the Lord and seek Him. God hears you and is a rewarder of those who diligently seek Him.

But without faith it is impossible to please Him, for he who comes to God must believe that He is, and that He is a rewarder of those who diligently seek Him (Hebrews 11:6 NKJV).

Sjhira Ellzey

My love I could never get bored or weary of just gazing at you. I gaze in wonder. I am intrigued. What in all the earth compares to your beauty? There is nothing. I could search for eternity and find nothing.

*

"I keep it by my bed. Every day I wake up and there it is for me to read. I just love it."
-Brianna (Bri)

*

Concise and simply stated by Bri. What a wonderful way to start your day; waking up and being reminded that Jesus is gazing in adoration at you. He's not asleep. He's not preoccupied with something else. He's not distracted. His eyes are fixed on His beloved. His eyes are fixed on you. Her response makes me think of the song, "Give Me Jesus."

In the morning, when I rise
In the morning, when I rise
In the morning, when I rise
Give me Jesus

Heart Expressions from the Throne Room

Give me Jesus

Give me Jesus

You can have all this world

Just give me Jesus

When I am alone

When I am alone

Oh, when I am alone

Give me Jesus

Give me Jesus

Give me Jesus

You can have all this world

Just give me Jesus

When I come to die

When I come to die

Oh, when I come to die

Give me Jesus

Give me Jesus

Give me Jesus

Sjhira Ellzey

You can have all this world
Just give me Jesus

You say you want to be loved? You say you want to be romanced and swept off your feet? Baby girl, I am love and the true lover of your soul. I created romance and I placed the desire in your heart to be swept off your feet. No one can love you like I love you. I want to be the one who wins your heart. Dare to ask me and watch how I take your breath away.

*

"If they only knew the love of Jesus they wouldn't be so mopey and depressed."
-Ellen

*

Ellen woke up Valentine's Day morning in a great mood. The entire day she watched her female peers get chocolates and flowers, and although this was the first Valentine's Day in years that Ellen didn't get anything from a guy she was content. In the past she would have felt differently.

As a young teenager, Ellen and a friend decided that a relationship with a guy equaled happiness. This mindset caused her to never be without a boyfriend since she was 16 years old. The reality of her happiness was constantly trying to make her boyfriend happy, i.e., if he didn't like a certain color she wouldn't wear it or if he didn't like the way she dressed she would alter it to his liking.

Ellen admitted that as a single woman growing in a deeper relationship with God, she felt better than ever. When she received her love note the night of February 14th her response was, "Aww, Jesus. I love you too!" The message to her was a reminder that Jesus' love is there for her every day and it was there before she was even born.

Ellen was able to tell her peers, from experience, that it's better to be single and in relationship with Jesus than to be in a relationship with the wrong guy at the wrong time and for the wrong reasons. That's a powerful message for anyone to hear!

I long for the day when I will crown you as my bride. I will be your king and you will be my queen and eternity will be ours. Together as one, nothing will stop us, come between us, or separate us. Your crown is a seal, we are one.

*

"...wow, that's deep. That's deeper than deep."
-Tasha

*

"When is my husband going to come? Who is he and what will he be like?" If we jumped inside Tasha's head leading up to Valentine's Day 2007, those are the questions we would have heard, over and over again. Tasha admitted that she focused on her future husband a lot. When she tried to focus on her relationship with the Lord, she was often discouraged because it seemed like people around her were advancing and she was not. Consequently, she felt "forgotten."

Reading God's message immediately shifted Tasha's focus from a natural husband to the Lord as her spiritual husband. With a smile on her face she exclaimed, "He is my groom. I am His bride."

Her feeling of being forgotten was replaced with the feeling of being desired. Tasha realized how much she had been obsessing over her future husband which caused her to miss the fact that God was right there in front of her. That could have been a large reason as to why she did not feel their relationship was advancing properly. With a sincere heart Tasha stated, "Even in the flesh, for someone to long for you is real nice...for God to long for me, wow, that's deep! That's deeper than deep."

There's nothing wrong with thinking about your future husband. That's very normal, and the desire comes from God. We just have to be careful not to make that desire an idol. If a woman places the idea of a husband or marriage as an idol, when the time comes for her to step into that glorious union designed by God, she won't be able to enjoy it. True fulfillment and satisfaction does not come from a spouse. That is something that should be learned as a single woman.

Knowing Jesus on a personal level is the only thing that fills us up to completion. When we experience a relationship with Him first, we will not be quick to run away from a difficult marriage or throw in the towel because of the imperfections of a husband. Instead, we will continue seeking Jesus in the good times and the bad times. With a heart fixed on Jesus, a husband/marriage will ignite a deeper longing and pursuit for the Father. Life on earth is temporary but life with Jesus is eternal.

So we fix our eyes not on what is seen, but on what is unseen, since what is seen is temporary, but what is unseen in eternal (2 Corinthians 4:18 NIV).

As conveyed in Tasha's love note, the Lord our God is the Bridegroom and we, the church, are His bride.

Sjhira Ellzey

Hold my hand. Draw close to me. Allow yourself to receive from me; my tender words, my loving gaze, my deep touch. Helplessly need me. Desperately long for me. I will not fail you. My sweetheart, you will not be disappointed.

*

"Even if He doesn't give me another romantic relationship I'm not going to be disappointed."
-Angelique

*

Angelique was expecting Valentine's Day to be filled with sadness. The relationship with her boyfriend of 3 years had recently ended, and she feared that she would never find another guy as good as him. Consequently, the sadness over her lost relationship triggered a deeper wound that Angelique shared with me; her struggle with "abandonment issues."

Angelique's father wasn't around and she lived life striving to be perfect to receive love. She confessed about her many tearful nights due to loneliness. Angelique was a beautiful, well spoken, well-educated young lady who carried herself with her shoulders back and her head held high. Looking at her from the outside one would never know how deep her pain went. Yet, she was suffering.

God knew about the sadness connected to the break-up and He also knew her pain had deeper roots. Nothing is hidden from the Lord. He sees and knows it all. Angelique read her love note and was moved that God saw her tears. What's amazing is that He didn't have to say that verbatim. His message spoke directly to disappointments that had caused her soul great anguish.

As He lovingly invited her to Him; to focus all her energy and attention on Him; to become vulnerable and weak before Him, His promise to her was that He would never fail her. What a poignant message for a young woman who had experienced years of disappointment and loneliness due to an absent father. Angelique confessed that the love note was, "building confidence in Him (God); in His love."

I have to stay here for a moment because as I am writing I can tangibly feel a weight on my heart. Again, the Holy Spirit wants to address the issue of Fatherlessness. It has become a norm. If one were to classify it as a disease, it has become a pandemic. It doesn't just mean a father who is MIA (missing in action) like Angelique's father, it can also be associated with abuse or stoicism and disengagement. Although I am emphasizing a man's role I want to be clear that a mother who is MIA or abusive or disengaged is just as detrimental to one's development. God's perfect design allows for a man and a woman to unite and take part in the miracle of life!

*God created man in his own image, in the image of God he created him; male and female he created them. God blessed them and said to them, be fruitful and increase in number...(*Genesis 1:27-28).

But He never intended for new life to come forth in the midst of chaos, confusion, and neglect. If our natural father is not a reflection of God the Father, like he should be, we will struggle to know our Creator. No wonder many people have difficulty with terms like, "Heavenly Father," and "God the Father." Our first introduction to love is supposed to be from our mother and father. God is love, therefore, our parents are our first direct understanding of who God is. Both mother and father reveal facets of God's character. They are equally important to a young person's growth in different ways.

If you are reading this with a heavy heart or you feel numb because your dad/mom has been a poor reflection of God's love, I want to extend hope. The Lord knows what you have experienced in your life that has created a wall or hurdle in getting to Him. He desires for you to know Him, and He knows how to tear down walls and remove hurdles. He knows how to pursue you.

But the Lord also wants you to be an active participant in His pursuit. He wants you to forgive. True healing awaits you but you must first let go of any bitterness, hatred, ill-will, etc.. towards your father (mother). I understand this may seem unfair, after all, why in the world would you forgive a person who hasn't shown remorse and doesn't deserve forgiveness? The simple answer is because God forgave you.

But instead be kind and affectionate toward one another. Has God graciously forgiven you? Then graciously forgive one another in the depths of Christ's love (Ephesians 4:32 TPT).

The key to forgiveness is realizing that a perfect and Holy God forgave us when we didn't deserve it; while we were still sinners. The other key to forgiveness is asking the Lord for help, especially when it seems unbearable. The love of Christ is powerful and knows no limits. With a grateful heart we first thank Jesus for forgiving our souls, and with that same heart of gratitude we extend forgiveness to others.

To be clear, forgiveness does not mean trust; that has to be earned. Forgiveness also doesn't mean a deep, warm, and fuzzy relationship automatically develops. In fact, you may never have that type of a relationship with your dad, or any other person you have forgiven, and that's ok! Because we are relational beings and He created the family structure, God knows how critical it is for you to have a healthy father/mother figure.

In your life, the Lord will place people before you that are reflectors of His character; people who know Him and allow His love to flow directly through them to you. You may already have people coming to mind that fit this description. Great! That's revelation from the Holy Spirit! Connect with them and soak up the love. Your relationship with these individuals will be a source of healing that your soul needs and longs for! Always remember that you are at the core of God's heart and He wants nothing less than for you to draw close to Him and enjoy Him as Abba…daddy…your Heavenly Father.

Sjhira Ellzey

You, my love, are radiant. As a ray of light peeks through the clouds and shines upon the earth, so does your soul radiate through the dark places in this world and touch the heart of man.

*

"After reading the note, I realized how much my cousin needed me."
-Dee Dee

*

Dee Dee received her love note on the eve of Valentine's Day and didn't read it until the following night. Needless to say, she wasn't that enthused about "a love note from Jesus." Her ex-boyfriend failed to say anything to her on Valentine's Day which caused her to be upset the entire day. Dee Dee was also dealing with the annoyance of a younger cousin who would call her often. Her cousin's mother was not around and she had no one to look up to, so she clung to Dee Dee. As many of us can relate, it's annoying when a younger sibling, family member, neighbor, or anyone is continuously needy for our attention. Dee

Dee admitted she was extremely annoyed and quick to get off the phone every time her cousin called.

When Dee Dee read her love note, the anger immediately lifted off of her and she said, "I was cool." The concept of light shining in darkness got her attention, and her thoughts went directly to her cousin. She knew her little cousin was in a dark place and needed "light." In that moment, Dee Dee had a dramatic change of heart as she realized the impact that was being made. From then on, she made an effort to call her cousin more often and stayed on the phone for as long as she was needed.

The selfless response to this love note warms my heart. Dee Dee didn't just receive a message from the Lord for her own feel-good experience, she was prompted to show love to another person. In her case, the recipient was not easy to love. In fact, she was needy and annoying, yet Dee Dee's heart was moved with compassion to be available for the sake of love. At the time, the only hope this young girl may have had was her big cousin. The Lord was loving this young girl through Dee Dee. How beautiful!

We are to be the hands, feet, and mouth of Jesus in a dark and dying world. His love compels us to love others and share the good news. This is why Jesus came to earth and chose disciples to carry out His message to all people.

But you shall receive power (ability, efficiency, and might) when the Holy Spirit has come upon you, and you shall be My witnesses in Jerusalem and all Judea and Samaria and to the ends (the very bounds) of the earth (Acts 1:8 AMPC).

Consider this, the Creator of all things chose *you* to be His mouthpiece on your college campus and beyond. As a believer and follower of Jesus, your name is known in Heaven and you have thousands upon thousands cheering for you. What a privilege and honor!

The enemy is tirelessly working to keep you unaware of the God-given mantle that rests on your shoulders. It's time to wake up! It's time to let the Holy Fire of God burn through you and light up your surroundings!

Heart Expressions from the Throne Room

In the same way, let your light shine before others, so that they may see your good works and give glory to your Father who is in heaven (Matthew 5:16).

A mystery to behold...when you walk away I follow. There is a part of me living inside of you and I cannot rest until we discover this truth together.

*

"God, let me help you out and take a load off your hands."
-Tori

*

Tori had a different reaction from most women. She read the note and thought it was for someone else. She was growing in a relationship with the Lord and this particular love note sounded like it was meant for someone "going astray" as she put it. That initial thought produced feelings of disappointment for Tori while her peers around her were experiencing true joy and delight.

My time with Tori was incredible as I heard her express a myriad of thoughts and emotions about this simple love note. She confessed that after some thought and prayer deeper meaning began to unravel and her starting point was with the word "truth."

The truth is, Tori struggled with her identity in Christ, which caused her to struggle with building peer relationships. She had a hard time connecting with the women in her dorm; not knowing how to be "cool" with them and still be different. She also mentioned that her roommate seemed fake and most guys acted like "gangsters." In her efforts to be "set apart" or different from the world, as the Bible teaches, Tori isolated herself from everyone. When she asked God for help He didn't seem to move fast enough and she would get impatient. As Tori said in her own words, she would interact with others or build relationships "on her terms," and go to God as her "fallback."

As the Lord opened her heart to deeper revelation she re-read her love note as it pertains to her relationships. The pattern of taking matters into her own hands and then going to God after her own way failed was an area of her life that the Lord was speaking to. Even when she tried to isolate herself, God was there. When she re-read, "a part of me is living inside of you," she thought about how God made her in His image, and when He lives in us we learn His character and our old selves become new, like Him. Therefore, we have love for ourselves and others because His love is inside of us.

This revelation helped Tori understand how much God cared about her relationships and her willingness to trust Him. She was still processing everything when we spoke, but it was a huge turn-around from her initially thinking the love note was meant for someone else.

I loved Tori's honesty! Her reaction was very real and relatable. The reality is, we have all felt disappointed by God and at times questioned His Word. As we grow in our relationship with Jesus we are allowed to access deeper chambers of His heart but it takes patience and time. It takes a willingness on our part to seek. He lovingly invites us to follow Him and then to seek Him. His Word says, *"You will seek me and find me when you seek me with all your heart. I will be found by you, declares the Lord,"* (Jeremiah 29:13 NIV).

Tori was disappointed when she received her love note, but instead of throwing it away or forgetting about it, she decided to pray and ask God why she received that particular note. Tori's story is a beautiful example of how we can all go before the Lord and seek Him for greater understanding, revelation, and wisdom. It is also a great reminder that God does not give up on us. When we walk away, trying to navigate this life in our own ability, there will be footsteps behind us. The moment we decide to stop, acknowledge that we are lost, and turn around, we will find that our answer is right there! He was there the entire time. Then we begin taking steps jointly in truth; in the way we were destined to go.

Sjhira Ellzey

PARTING WORDS

Was that a delicious meal or what? Even though you just ate a lot of food, that was only a small fraction of what the marriage supper of the Lamb will be like! I know it may be tempting to sit back, loosen the button on your pants and go into a comatose state, but we don't have time for that! We have work to do!

The Lord's plan for you to have this in your hands was set in motion before the foundation of the world. Tears of joy, prayers of redemption, declarations of healing, and songs of hope were sown into this book, and by the power of the Living God there will be a great harvest! You were chosen for such a time as this to be a part of this great harvest.

College campuses all over the world are filled with people who are crying out for love and truth. Whether this is your first year, last year, or somewhere in between, don't let this precious time pass you by. This is your moment to make a generational impact!

So, let's do it! Let's use our faith to cause Heaven and earth to shake and cause demons to tremble with fear. Let's pledge our allegiance to the King of kings and the Lord of lords. Let's walk together, united with one voice, and boldly declare the Good News! Above all else, let us continue to seek the face of our Lord so that everything we do is for love.

If I could speak all the languages of earth and of angels, but didn't love others, I would only be a noisy gong or a clanging cymbal. If I had the gift of prophecy, and if I understood all of God's secret plans and possessed all knowledge, and if I had such faith that I could move mountains, but didn't love others, I would be nothing. If I gave everything I have to the poor and even sacrificed my body, I could boast about; but if I didn't love others, I would have gained nothing. Love is patient and kind. Love is not jealous or boastful or proud or rude. It does not demand its own way. It is not irritable, and it keeps no record of being wronged. It does not rejoice about injustice but rejoices whenever the truth wins out. Love never gives up, never loses faith, is always hopeful, and endures through every circumstance. Three things will last forever - faith, hope, and love - and the greatest of these is love (1Corinthians 13:1-7, 13 NLT).

    I thank God for you and I pray you will continue receiving His Heart Expressions from the Throne Room; that you will be a living testimony of Jesus' heart for His beloved. If we don't get a chance to meet on this side of eternity, I look forward to our reunion in Glory! May Jehovah bless you and keep you. May Jehovah make His face to shine upon you and be gracious to you. May Jehovah lift up His countenance upon you and give you peace. Amen.

ABOUT THE AUTHOR

Sjhira Ellzey has had a tender heart before the Lord and a desire to know Him since she was a little girl. Before she was conceived, her mother had a dream that she was holding a baby girl and the baby's name was "Jhira," pronounced ji-rah. Sometime later her mother became pregnant and after a very difficult, hi-risk pregnancy, including 5 months of bed rest, and 18-hours of labor that ended in a cesarean, Sjhira (with a silent "S" because her father wanted the family initials to be the same) was born.

When she was an infant her mother was watching Christian television and heard them singing Sjhira's name. She discovered there was a name for God in the Bible that means: The Lord will provide; provision - Jehovah Jireh, and immediately knew that her dream was from the Lord! Sjhira has carried this story in her heart most of her life and knows that she has great purpose for being on earth at this time. No matter what she is doing, Sjhira has a burning desire to help others: realize they were known by God before conception as recorded in Jeremiah 1:5, re-connect with their Creator; enjoying a dynamic love relationship, and living out their God-given purpose with conviction, passion, and joy!

While pursing pre-med at Vanderbilt University, the Lord called Sjhira into vocational campus ministry. During her junior year she changed her major to Communication Studies and upon graduating moved to California where she completed some graduate work at Fuller Theological Seminary.

After working a short season in full-time ministry, the Lord had more surprises for her and, what may seem to some as a random path, the Lord has been leading her through every twist and turn for a truly exhilarating ride. As a new author, she is thrilled that publishing a book has been a part of this exciting journey! Sjhira currently resides in Tennessee with her husband, Kyndl, and their very busy toddler son who fills their hearts with so much joy. To learn more, visit www.sjhiraellzey.com.

www.ingramcontent.com/pod-product-compliance
Lightning Source LLC
Chambersburg PA
CBHW071302110426
42743CB00042B/1150